BAPTISTWAY®

Adult Bible Study Guide

2 Corinthians

Taking Ministry Personally

Wilma Reed
Phil Lineberger
Dennis Foust

BAPTISTWAY PRESS®
Dallas, Texas

BAPTISTWAY PRESS® Management Team
Executive Director, Baptist General Convention of Texas: Charles Wade
Coordinator, Church Health and Growth Section: H. Lynn Eckeberger
Director, Bible Study/Discipleship Center: Dennis Parrott

Publishing consultant: Ross West, Positive Difference Communications
Cover and Interior Design and Production: Desktop Miracles, Inc.
Cover Photo: Scene from ancient Corinth, BiblePlaces.com

First edition: September 2004
ISBN: 1–931060–51–7

How to Make the Best Use of This Issue

Whether you're the teacher or a student—

1. Start early in the week before your class meets.
2. Overview the study. Review the table of contents and read the study introduction. Try to see how each lesson relates to the overall study.
3. Use your Bible to read and consider prayerfully the Scripture passages for the lesson. (You'll see that each writer has chosen a favorite translation for the lessons in this issue. You're free to use the Bible translation you prefer and compare it with the translation chosen for that unit, of course.)
4. After reading all the Scripture passages in your Bible, then read the writer's comments. The comments are intended to be an aid to your study of the Bible.
5. Read the small articles—"sidebars"—in each lesson. They are intended to provide additional, enrichment information and inspiration and to encourage thought and application.
6. Try to answer for yourself the questions included in each lesson. They're intended to encourage further thought and application, and they can also be used in the class session itself.

If you're the teacher—

A. Do all of the things just mentioned, of course.
B. In the first session of the study, briefly overview the study by identifying with your class the date on which each lesson will be studied. Lead your class to write the date in the table of contents on page 5 and on the first page of each lesson. You might also find it helpful to make and post a chart that indicates the date on which each lesson will be studied. If all of your class has e-mail, send them an e-mail with the dates the lessons will be studied. (At least one church that uses BAPTISTWAY® materials for its classes places a sticker on the table of contents to identify the dates.)
C. Get a copy of the *Teaching Guide*, a companion piece to this *Study Guide*. The *Teaching Guide* contains additional Bible comments plus two teaching plans. The teaching plans in the *Teaching Guide* are

intended to provide practical, easy-to-use teaching suggestions that will work in your class.

D. After you've studied the Bible passage, the lesson comments, and other material, use the teaching suggestions in the *Teaching Guide* to help you develop your plan for leading your class in studying each lesson.

E. You may want to get the additional adult Bible study comments— *Adult Online Bible Commentary*—by Dr. Jim Denison, pastor of Park Cities Baptist Church, Dallas, Texas, that are available at *www. baptistwaypress.org* and can be downloaded free. An additional teaching plan plus teaching resource items are also available at *www.baptistwaypress.org.*

F. You also may want to get the enrichment teaching help that is provided in the *Baptist Standard*, in either the printed or the internet editions. Call 214–630–4571 to begin your subscription to the *Baptist Standard.* Access the internet information by checking the *Baptist Standard* website at *http://www.baptiststandard.com.* (Other class participants may find this information helpful, too.)

G. Enjoy leading your class in discovering the meaning of the Scripture passages and in applying these passages to their lives.

2 Corinthians: Taking Ministry Personally

UNIT ONE

Ministering to People Who Disagree

Date of Study

UNIT TWO

Learning to Give

UNIT THREE

Getting Beyond the Status Quo

Introducing

2 CORINTHIANS:
Taking Ministry Personally

The Letter of 2 Corinthians is part of Paul's correspondence with what might well have been the most troublesome church he founded. Paul had founded the church at Corinth on his second missionary journey (Acts 18:1–17). Corinth, a seaport, was a cosmopolitan city. Its morals or lack of them were so well known that *to corinthianize* was a euphemism for sexual debauchery. Thus, although Paul began the church out of the synagogue, many of the Corinthian believers likely were from the rawest of pagan backgrounds. So the church's first members were hardly the kind of Baptist deacon family that most Baptist churches today would refer to as "good prospects"! Therefore, it is no wonder that 1 Corinthians revealed the church at Corinth to have been plagued by numerous problems. The problems continued in 2 Corinthians, but the emphasis shifted to a challenge to Paul's leadership. Thus, much of 2 Corinthians deals with Paul's defense of his ministry in general and his right to minister to the Corinthian church in particular.

In some ways, 2 Corinthians is Paul's most personal letter, revealing more of himself and more personal details than any of his other letters. Over and over Paul sought ways to persuade the Corinthians to return to loyalty to him. Somehow rival teachers were drawing the church away from appreciation of Paul and attention to his instructions, to the detriment of the church. Exactly who these rival teachers were and what they taught, we do not know. What we do know is that they were in the process of convincing the Corinthians that Paul was second-rate as compared to them. Evidently much more was involved than a popularity contest. Rather, Paul was concerned about the direction these rival teachers were leading the Corinthians. Paul believed that the Corinthian church's attraction to these rival leaders was damaging to the church. Thus he used various means to try to remedy the situation so that he and the Corinthians could repair the rift between them.

Second Corinthians is unlike any other of Paul's letters. It is not like Romans, Paul's most heavily-reasoned explanation of the gospel. It is not even like 1 Corinthians, which offers explanations of ethical and theological issues that the church at Corinth was concerned about. Unlike these and other Pauline letters, 2 Corinthians does not contain an extensive theological section followed by an extensive ethical section. Rather, 2 Corinthians begins and ends with a defense by Paul of his apostolic ministry (chapters 1—7, 10—13). A small middle section encouraged the Corinthians to participate in the offering for the saints in Jerusalem that Paul was leading in collecting (chapters 8—9). Moreover, 2 Corinthians contains numerous references to Paul's life and to his personal feelings (see, for example, 1:3–10, 23–24; 2:1–14; 5:6–11; 6:3–12; 7:2–15; 11:22–29). Perhaps 2 Corinthians is more like we think a letter to be than Paul's other letters are. Like some personal letters today, 2 Corinthians tends to jump from topic to topic and back again.

Additional Resources for Studying 2 Corinthians[3]
Paul Barnett. *The Second Epistle to the Corinthians.* The New International Commentary on the New Testament. Grand Rapids, Michigan: William B. Eerdmans Publishing Company, 1997.
G.R. Beasley-Murray. "2 Corinthians." *The Broadman Bible Commentary.* Volume 11. Nashville, Tennessee: Broadman Press, 1971.
Ernest Best. *Second Corinthians.* Interpretation: A Bible Commentary for Teaching and Preaching. Louisville: John Knox Press, 1987.
F.F. Bruce. *1 and 2 Corinthians.* New Century Bible. London: Oliphants, 1971.
Kenneth L. Chafin. *1, 2 Corinthians.* The Communicator's Commentary. Waco, Texas: Word Books, Publisher, 1985.
David Garland. *2 Corinthians.* The New American Commentary. Nashville, Tennessee: Broadman and Holman, 1999.
Brian Harbour. *2 Corinthians: Commissioned to Serve.* Nashville, Tennessee: Convention Press, 1989.
Ralph P. Martin. *2 Corinthians.* Word Biblical Commentary. Volume 40. Waco, Texas: Word Books Publisher, 1986.
John B. Polhill. *Paul and His Letters.* Nashville, Tennessee: Broadman and Holman Publishers, 1999.
A.T. Robertson. *Word Pictures in the New Testament.* Volume IV. Nashville, Tennessee: Broadman Press, 1931.
J. Paul Sampley. "The Second Letter to the Corinthians." *The New Interpreter's Bible.* Volume XI. Nashville: Abingdon Press, 2000.

In writing 2 Corinthians, Paul used the communication skills of that day to try to persuade the Corinthians to return to the friendship that had once bound them together. One of these methods, familiar in that time, was called "frank speech." In using "frank speech," a person would seek to encourage a friend to make improvement in some way or other. As is readily apparent, "frank speech" is sometimes necessary but generally always risky, no matter what century it is when it is used! The words needed to be spoken in just the right tone and at just the right moment, and always out of concern for the friend. Paul referred directly to this method in 6:11.

Another method was "self-commendation." We see plenty of people engaging in "self-commendation" these days, but most folks still are uncomfortable with the very idea. The method was acceptable in that day, however, if done with just the right touch of humility, avoiding arrogance.[1] Paul believed his opponents had crossed the line, and he carefully pointed out to the Corinthians that they themselves were his "letters of recommendation" (3:1).[2]

While we call this letter 2 Corinthians, it in reality is only the second letter that we have. If we had all the letters mentioned, 2 Corinthians would be at least "4 Corinthians." A letter earlier than 1 Corinthians is mentioned in 1 Corinthians 5:9. Too, between 1 Corinthians and 2 Corinthians was another letter, also lost, that caused pain to the Corinthians and on which Paul was following up in 2 Corinthians (see 2 Cor. 2:2–3; 7:8). In addition, some Bible interpreters consider 2 Corinthians itself to be composed of more than one letter in light of the shift in tone between 2 Corinthians 1—9 and 2 Corinthians 10—13. All the manuscript evidence has the two parts together as 2 Corinthians, however.

In light of the personal nature of 2 Corinthians, many of the lessons to be studied will focus on personal issues for us, too. Such personal issues to be considered during this study include these: facing suffering; comforting others; overcoming strained relationships; ministering to others; not losing heart; facing death; being authentic; giving our poooooiono; dealing with conflict; relying on God's grace; and considering how to help people, especially people we love, to change.

2 CORINTHIANS: *Taking Ministry Personally*

UNIT ONE, MINISTERING TO PEOPLE WHO DISAGREE

Lesson 1	When You Suffer	2 Corinthians 1:1–11
Lesson 2	When Relationships Are Strained	2 Corinthians 1:12—2:11
Lesson 3	Measuring Our Ministry	2 Corinthians 2:14—3:6
Lesson 4	Maintaining Heart for Ministry	2 Corinthians 4:1–15
Lesson 5	Confidence for Now and Forever	2 Corinthians 4:16—5:10
Lesson 6	Motivated to Minister	2 Corinthians 5:11–21
Lesson 7	Be Faithful, Be Real	2 Corinthians 6:1–13; 7:2–4
Lesson 8	Giving and Receiving Criticism	2 Corinthians 7:5–16

UNIT TWO, LEARNING TO GIVE

Lesson 9	Reasons for Giving	2 Corinthians 8:1–21
Lesson 10	Blessings of Giving	2 Corinthians 9:6–15

UNIT THREE, GETTING BEYOND THE STATUS QUO

Lesson 11	Dealing with Conflict	2 Corinthians 10
Lesson 12	Grace Sufficient	2 Corinthians 12:1–10
Lesson 13	On Trying to Change People	2 Corinthians 12:14—13:13

NOTES

1. J. Paul Sampley, "The Second Letter to the Corinthians," *The New Interpreter's Bible*, vol. XI (Nashville: Abingdon Press, 2000), 29–30.
2. Unless otherwise indicated, all Scripture quotations in "Introducing 2 Corinthians" are from the New Revised Standard Version.
3. Listing a book does not imply full agreement by the writers or BAPTISTWAY PRESS® with all of its comments.

Ministering to People Who Disagree

This unit deals with 2 Corinthians 1—7 and consists of eight lessons. In this portion of 2 Corinthians, Paul carefully but energetically defended himself and his ministry.

Rival teachers had capitalized on a misunderstanding of previous instructions from Paul and what the Corinthians considered to be a broken promise by Paul about visiting them. The result was a serious "chip-on-the-shoulder" attitude on the part of the Corinthians. This problem had escalated into a troubling breach in the church's relationship with Paul.

As with personal letters even today, the emphasis shifts back and forth from one thing to another rather than being like an essay that treats one point fully and then moves to the next point. The lessons aim at following the contours of the Bible passages and seek to emphasize Paul's message. That is the main reason this unit of study is lengthier than units of study generally are. The subject matter in these seven chapters is similar. Thus, to divide the unit into two or more units would be arbitrary.

Paul sought to draw the Corinthians back to a positive relationship with him. These lessons focus on Paul's approach to the Corinthians in achieving this goal, and they develop applications to current personal and church life.[1]

11

UNIT ONE: MINISTERING TO PEOPLE WHO DISAGREE

NOTES

1. Unless otherwise indicated, all Scripture quotations in unit one are from The Holy Bible, New International Version (North American Edition), copyright © 1973, 1978, 1984 by the International Bible Society. Used by permission of Zondervan Publishing House.

Focal Text

2 Corinthians 1:1–11

Background

2 Corinthians 1:1–11

Main Idea

Our experiences of suffering can become avenues for recognizing God's faithfulness and extending help to others.

Question to Explore

When difficulties come, what can we do?

Study Aim

To summarize Paul's approach to the suffering he experienced and identify implications for my life

Study and Action Emphases

- Affirm the Bible as our authoritative guide for life and ministry
- Develop a growing, vibrant faith
- Include all God's family in decision-making and service
- Value all people as created in the image of God
- Obey and serve Jesus by meeting physical, spiritual, and emotional needs
- Equip people for servant leadership

LESSON ONE

When You Suffer

Quick Read

Paul affirmed the sufficiency of God's comfort in times of suffering.

A puzzling message popped up on my computer screen. It read: "Mom, didn't you mean Happy Anniversary, Sunday? Anyway, thanks for the $100." I have no idea who sent the e-mail or for whom it was intended. It was a misdirected communiqué.

The custom in Paul's day left no room for such errors. Long ago letters followed a standard form much as some letters do today. The salutation included the writer's name and the audience for whom the correspondence was intended. Paul addressed this letter primarily to the church in Corinth.

Some preachers and Christian workers like to travel incognito. They try to not give a hint about their work or their calling because they think they are more likely to gain an entree to witness if their contacts do not know they are ministers. Paul, though, readily disclosed who he was and what his apostolic calling was in the salutation of every one of his letters.

2 Corinthians 1:1–11

[1]Paul, an apostle of Christ Jesus by the will of God, and Timothy our brother,

To the church of God in Corinth, together with all the saints throughout Achaia:

[2]Grace and peace to you from God our Father and the Lord Jesus Christ.

[3]Praise be to the God and Father of our Lord Jesus Christ, the Father of compassion and the God of all comfort, [4]who comforts us in all our troubles, so that we can comfort those in any trouble with the comfort we ourselves have received from God. [5]For just as the sufferings of Christ flow over into our lives, so also through Christ our comfort overflows. [6]If we are distressed, it is for your comfort and salvation; if we are comforted, it is for your comfort, which produces in you patient endurance of the same sufferings we suffer. [7]And our hope for you is firm, because we know that just as you share in our sufferings, so also you share in our comfort.

[8]We do not want you to be uninformed, brothers, about the hardships we suffered in the province of Asia. We were under great pressure, far beyond our ability to endure, so that we despaired even of life. [9]Indeed, in our hearts we felt the sentence of death. But this happened that we might not rely on ourselves but on God, who raises the dead. [10]He has delivered us from such a deadly peril, and he will deliver us. On him we have set our hope that he will continue to deliver us, [11]as you help us by your prayers. Then many will give thanks on our behalf for the gracious favor granted us in answer to the prayers of many.

Introducing 2 Corinthians

Bible scholars generally agree that this is the most personal of Paul's letters. Whereas his other epistles dealt with theological and ethical subjects, this letter is more autobiographical. Paul gave us glimpses of his theology and ministry in this letter. Unfortunately, he omitted information that was probably known to his readers but that might have helped us understand the letter better. Our lack of this information complicates our understanding and leaves us wondering.

By intercessory prayer the newest Christian can have a part in God's redemptive work

Corinth was an international city, the leading business center of ancient Greece. It was a shipping route between the Adriatic and Aegean Seas. Trade flowed back and forth from Egypt, Asia Minor, Syria, and Italy, thus introducing a stream of intellectual and religious influences. Popular proverbs describing its wealth and licentiousness were common talk.

The great temple of Aphrodite was in Corinth. The influence of this goddess was widespread throughout the ancient world. In Corinth, the myth was held that this Greek goddess rose from the sea. Her maritime connections made her thousand priestesses and religious prostitutes especially popular among the hundreds of transient sailors who visited the city.

Paul first visited Corinth around A.D. 50 (Acts 18:1) while on his second missionary journey. He made many disciples and founded the church. He stayed about eighteen months (Acts 18:11) before returning to Antioch in Syria where he ended his tour. During the year and a half Paul was in Corinth, he taught the new converts, and the new converts certainly needed teaching! Although Paul probably began the church out of the synagogue, people with the rawest pagan backgrounds were won to the Lord. They needed his spiritual insights, wise counsel, and tender love. Paul felt that since he had established the church, he had a responsibility to continue in its nurture and guidance. This he did through visits and letters.

Salutation and Doxology (1:1–3)

Having stated his authority as an apostle, Paul often named another person or other people who were with him. Earlier Timothy, Paul's "son in the faith" (1 Timothy 1:2) and coworker, had been dispatched to Corinth to evaluate the situation (1 Corinthians 4:17). At this writing, Timothy was back with Paul. Circumstances had improved, but there were still opposing factions who refused to recognize Paul's authority.

An array of scholars feel Paul's reference to his apostleship in 2 Corinthians was a direct effort to refute his critics' claims that he failed to meet certain criteria to be recognized as an apostle. Piecing together bits and pieces of information, Bible commentators believe this may be Paul's fourth letter to the Corinthian church (see "Introducing 2 Corinthians"). They reason a preceding letter was a stern rebuke because serious quarrels had developed in the fellowship during his absence (2 Cor. 2:3). Some denied Paul's authority. They questioned his credibility in claiming to be an apostle since he was not associated with Jesus during Jesus' earthly ministry. They discredited Paul's role because he had no formal letters of recommendation from any Christian community.

Bible scholars generally agree that this is the most personal of Paul's letters.

Paul, on the other hand, thought his personal visit from the risen Lord on the road to Damascus (Acts 9:1–6) and perhaps his subsequent vision (Acts 18:9–11) could be compared to the disciples' being with Jesus during his time on earth. Paul thought his sufferings for Christ were sufficient to set him apart as an apostle. He insisted his call and commission were valid because he received them from the Lord himself (Galatians 1:1). He was explicit when he said he never sought or gained official approval from anyone. In his opinion, he didn't need it. He considered his suffering for Christ was yet another validation of his apostleship.

Paul felt that since he had established the church, he had a responsibility to continue in its nurture and guidance.

The custom of the day was for the writer to express a gracious attitude or wish for the recipients. Paul's use of the formality was no superficial conformity. He expanded the accepted form to convey, as he did in every letter, a message of faith. The reference to "grace and peace to you from God our Father and the Lord Jesus Christ" (2 Cor. 1:2) was intended to remind his readers of God's beneficence in the face of their unworthiness.

"Grace" refers to God's unmerited favor. Grace describes both God's attitude and action whereby God forgives undeserving sinners and restores

Case Study

Some time ago, a foreign government seized two Baptist missionaries on false charges and imprisoned them. Some days the prisoners were forced to stand for hours under the mid-day sun, with their arms extended over their heads. The younger man thought his malaria-ridden body could stand it no longer, but he became preoccupied watching his elderly co-worker standing stalwart. Unseen hands seemed to be holding him up. It was the older man's birthday! Thousands of Christians were praying for him since his name was on their calendar of prayer. How would concerted prayer impact the ministry of your church?

them to a love relationship with himself. Grace is God's effort to bring hopelessly alienated humanity into harmony with God's will. Grace cannot be earned or bestowed by another person. It is a free gift that can only be accepted. Once accepted, it initiates a changed life. A right relationship with God under the influence of the Holy Spirit produces right conduct. Composer Julia H. Johnston captured the essence of grace in her beloved hymn, "Grace Greater than Our Sin." She described its abundance and power, concluding it is "marvelous, infinite, matchless."[1]

Paul expanded his desire for the believers to include "peace." What is the peace Paul intended his readers to experience? Peace is an inner tranquility independent of circumstances. It cannot exist apart from grace. It cannot be imitated or counterfeited. It is not elusive or intermittent. It is a constant in the believer's life. It is a composure that passes understanding (Philippians 4:7).

Grace is God's effort to bring hopelessly alienated humanity into harmony with God's will.

Neither grace nor peace can be earned. They are gifts possible only in Jesus. Jesus said, "Peace I leave with you; my peace I give to you, I do not give to you as the world gives. Do not let your hearts be troubled and do not be afraid" (John 14:27). Peace comes from being centered in God's will. It is confident assurance of God's good intentions toward God's own. To experience this peace is to eliminate worry and fear from life because God is good, and God is in control.

The mere recollection of such graciousness prompted Paul to an interlude of praise. He wrote, "Praise be to the God and Father of our Lord Jesus Christ, the Father of compassion and the God of all comfort" (2 Cor. 3:3).

The Ministry of Suffering and Comfort (1:4–10)

In God's grand economy of life, nothing is wasted, not even suffering. Divine comfort is an enabling that extends beyond the sufferer to other people. Although usually not immediate, suffering can turn into blessings in time.

A right relationship with God under the influence of the Holy Spirit produces right conduct.

Paul viewed tribulation and suffering as a stewardship. In his mind, trouble and comfort are like two sides of a coin. One side was painful; the other, rewarding. One side was awful; the other, joyful. One side yielded misery; the other, ministry. Each sorrow equips the bearer to lend spiritual aid to someone else. Having experienced God's consolation ourselves, we can extend strength, hope, and encouragement to others who are undergoing trials.

Many years ago our infant daughter was critically ill. There were times when it appeared she might not survive. On one of those occasions, a woman from our church whom I barely knew came to visit. "I know what you are going through," she said, "When my little girl was about your baby's age she became ill." Somehow I knew of all our visitors that mother really did understand our terrible plight. Her suffering was my blessing. Thankfully, our daughter survived.

A Church Letter

Baptist worship services usually include an "invitation." It is a time when those moved by God to do so are invited to make a public decision. They may repent, rededicate themselves, and/or ask to join the fellowship by baptism, statement, or letter. Baptism occurs only once—upon repentance and profession of faith in Christ. The person then becomes a member of the church.

A person joining by statement has already been baptized but wants to unite with a sister church. The person is received by statement if the record of the prospective member's previous affiliation is not available. In receiving the person in this manner, the receiving church should be satisfied the applicant is trustworthy. By vote of the congregation, the person may become a member.

A church letter is a communication between churches "of like faith and order." The prospective member responds to the invitation by asking for membership "on promise of a letter." The receiving church contacts the former church for information about the person's previous membership. The former church votes to grant the letter that will affirm or deny the person's Christian character, conduct, and membership.

While the principle of stewardship applies to all suffering, Paul was writing about a particular kind of suffering: suffering as a Christian. It was neither a new nor novel idea for the roving missionary. His sufferings came as no surprise (Acts 9:16). They were expected! Pious Jews believed great suffering was a prerequisite to Messiah's coming. Indeed there *was* great suffering, but Jesus did it. He suffered instead of the people. He was the Suffering Servant whom Isaiah described in graphic detail (Isaiah 53). He suffered for us! Not only did Jesus suffer *for* us, but Jesus also suffers *with* us (Acts 9:4–5).

Paul was an authority on suffering, and that made him an authority on comfort also.

He never viewed suffering as a misfortune but rather a privilege. He felt it created a spiritual union with Christ that could be acquired in no other way. Paul felt that he and Christ were bonded more closely because the Lord suffered *with* him. Paul learned that as surely as serving Christ brought great suffering, Christ's moment-by-moment consolation was far greater (2 Cor. 1:5).

For Paul, all of his suffering fell in two categories: personal blessings and benefits to the church. Paul explained that his suffering actually worked out not only for his good but to their advantage as well because they had his experience as their example.

While we cannot be sure of the danger Paul confronted, the Corinthians apparently were aware of the incident but not the severity. Speculation suggests Paul was referring to fighting "with wild beasts" at Ephesus (1 Cor. 15:32) or to the riot there (Acts 19:23–36). Whatever the circumstances, Paul despaired of his life. The situation was so excruciating he thought he might be killed, and there was nothing he could do to save himself. He was utterly dependent on the Lord. He counted even that a blessing because he came to terms with death. Like Abraham of Old Testament times (Genesis 22:1–24), he believed God had the power to overcome death and restore him to life if that were God's plan (2 Cor. 1:10). Having withstood such peril, Paul was certain his never-changing God would sustain him in all future dangers. The entire incident was a trial he endured for the name of Christ (Acts 9:16). He was confident God would do no less on his behalf in the future than God had done in the past.

Peace is an inner tranquility independent of circumstances.

19

I once heard a missionary say that where she worked, the believers were so committed to taking the gospel to the surrounding hostile villages that each messenger had two or three volunteers who served as back-ups. The Christians, determined to witness to the neighboring pagan tribes, went gladly, believing they would be killed. Yet they were consoled that others were ready to take their places and reach the lost.

God, however, delivered Paul from his dreadful ordeal. We do not know how, but clearly it was by divine intervention. Prayer also had a part in his deliverance. He believed the Corinthians themselves had participated in his survival. Their prayers were a factor in his rescue. He went through great peril and came out triumphant. In these verses, Paul reminded the Corinthians of what he had experienced (1:8–10).

Ministry of Intercessory Prayer (1:11)

Paul was a person of prayer. He was a faithful intercessor (Phil. 1:1–5; Colossians 1:3). He had great faith in the power of prayer (Romans 15:30–31; Phil. 1:19; Col. 4:12). So he called on the believers to continue to pray for him and his coworkers. He saw the prayer ministry of the church as another occasion for mutual benefit: the more people praying, the more rejoicing there would be when the answers came. By intercessory prayer the newest Christian can have a part in God's redemptive work

Huis Egge is a ninety-one-year-old woman who prays for missionaries daily. She has more than 150 names on her prayer list. Her intercessory praying began at least forty years ago. In some cases, she began praying for missionary appointees as soon as they announced their calling. She continued to pray for them throughout their careers on the mission field. She still prays for them in their retirement years. About thirty-five years ago she began writing weekly letters to missionaries, letting them know she was praying for them. Now with e-mail, she faithfully continues her ministry of letters and prayer. What a reward awaits that dear lady when she gets to heaven!

In God's grand economy of life, nothing is wasted, not even suffering.

Paul Can Be Our Mentor, Too

What can we learn from Paul when we are faced with suffering? We can grow spiritually from it and then use our experience to comfort others who are suffering. We can be assured God is with us.

QUESTIONS

1. How did Paul show his love for the Corinthians?

2. How was Paul's ministry different from that of the other apostles?

3. Why do Christians suffer?

4. How is suffering for Christ different from suffering in general?

NOTES

1. "Grace Greater Than Our Sin," words by Julia H. Johnston, 1849–1919.

Focal Text

2 Corinthians 1:12—2:11

Background

2 Corinthians 1:12—2:13

Main Idea

We are to respond in a Christian manner when relationships with other people are strained.

Question to Explore

How do you handle strained relationships with others?

Study Aim

To evaluate how I deal with strained relationships

Study and Action Emphases

- Affirm the Bible as our authoritative guide for life and ministry
- Develop a growing, vibrant faith
- Include all God's family in decision-making and service
- Value all people as created in the image of God
- Equip people for servant leadership

LESSON TWO

When Relationships Are Strained

Quick Read

Paul defended his ministry and the changes in his itinerary. He dealt with church discipline and with Christ as the fulfillment of God's Messianic promises.

For decades Abigail Van Buren, otherwise known as "Dear Abby," has provided advice to perplexed people. Her correspondents have sought help with twisted and broken relationships. Frequently, readers offer suggestions, and the columnist passes along a variety of possible solutions.

Who hasn't endured a strained or severed relationship? What is a person to do? Paul was an authority on strained and broken relationships, as he was with suffering for Christ and experiencing God's sustaining comfort. He was experiencing strained relationships with the Corinthian church, which prompted him to write 2 Corinthians.

2 Corinthians 1:12—2:11

[12]Now this is our boast: Our conscience testifies that we have conducted ourselves in the world, and especially in our relations with you, in the holiness and sincerity that are from God. We have done so not according to worldly wisdom but according to God's grace. [13]For we do not write you anything you cannot read or understand. And I hope that, [14]as you have understood us in part, you will come to understand fully that you can boast of us just as we will boast of you in the day of the Lord Jesus.

[15]Because I was confident of this, I planned to visit you first so that you might benefit twice. [16]I planned to visit you on my way to Macedonia and to come back to you from Macedonia, and then to have you send me on my way to Judea. [17]When I planned this, did I do it lightly? Or do I make my plans in a worldly manner so that in the same breath I say, "Yes, yes" and "No, no"?

[18]But as surely as God is faithful, our message to you is not "Yes" and "No." [19]For the Son of God, Jesus Christ, who was preached among you by me and Silas and Timothy, was not "Yes" and "No," but in him it has always been "Yes." [20]For no matter how many promises God has made, they are "Yes" in Christ. And so through him the "Amen" is spoken by us to the glory of God. [21]Now it is God who makes both us and you stand firm in Christ. He anointed us, [22]set his seal of ownership on us, and put his Spirit in our hearts as a deposit, guaranteeing what is to come. [2:1]So I made up my mind that I would not make another painful visit to you.

[2:2]For if I grieve you, who is left to make me glad but you whom I have grieved? [3]I wrote as I did so that when I came I should not be distressed by those who ought to make me rejoice. I had confidence in all of you, that you would all share my joy. [4]For I wrote you out of great distress and anguish of heart and with many tears, not to grieve you but to let you know the depth of my love for you.

> [5] If anyone has caused grief, he has not so much grieved me as he has grieved all of you, to some extent—not to put it too severely. [6] The punishment inflicted on him by the majority is sufficient for him. [7] Now instead, you ought to forgive and comfort him, so that he will not be overwhelmed by excessive sorrow. [8] I urge you, therefore, to reaffirm your love for him. [9] The reason I wrote you was to see if you would stand the test and be obedient in everything. [10] If you forgive anyone, I also forgive him. And what I have forgiven—if there was anything to forgive—I have forgiven in the sight of Christ for your sake, [11] in order that Satan might not outwit us. For we are not unaware of his schemes.

When Boasting Isn't Bragging (1:12–14)

Having expressed appreciation for the church's prayers for him (1:11), Paul next defended his character in no uncertain terms. His conscience was clear, and his motives were pure. Paul contended his ministry among them was above reproach. His intentions were holy and sincere. Therefore, criticism of him or his ministry was unwarranted.

Self-commendation was a literary form used in Paul's day. To us, the technique sounds arrogant and conceited. We think self-grandiosity conflicts with Jesus' words and example of self-lessness and humility, but Paul contended that the Corinthian Christians of all people should know his ministry was unblemished.

Who hasn't endured a strained or severed relationship?

Probably every teacher knows that reading, hearing, and understanding are entirely individual experiences. Just because a person can hear words or read them does not mean the person comprehends their meaning. Paul addressed a similar problem among the Corinthians. Either some of the people understood and some did not, or none of them fully understood what Paul expected of them. He wanted everyone to understand completely.

Paul lived his life with one eye on the present and one eye on the future (Philippians 1:21). He was confident that in the final judgment everyone would appear before the judgment seat of Christ, where every secret thought and action would be exposed. With his characteristic confidence, he believed both he and the Corinthians would pass the Lord's intense scrutiny. He would then be vindicated and the church would find nothing shameful about his life or ministry. Likewise, he would have no

25

disappointment in them. He reasoned that if such mutual appreciation were possible in the future, they could experience it in the present if they fully understood him.

Defending a Change in Plans (1:15—2:4)

Paul had some explaining to do about his on-again, off-again visits. He explained that he had intended to visit the church en route to Macedonia and to visit them again on his return trek (1:15–16). Evidently he had originally planned to come to Corinth only once (1 Corinthians 16:5). At the time of his planning, likely he assumed the church dissension would be settled and everyone would be glad to see him. But things were not settled. He could not be sure the waiting church would be glad to see him at all.

All of Paul's travel plans to and from Corinth are not clear from the information we have. Somehow, though, after further consideration and, no doubt, prayer, he changed his travel plans and decided against making a return visit (2 Cor. 1:23; 2:1). He wrote this letter instead.

Paul's detractors used his itinerary changes as fodder to feed their argument that he was fickle, hypocritical, and wishy-washy. They accused him of double-talk, saying *yes* and meaning *no* or saying *no* and meaning *yes*.

Some people are masters at double-talk. Long before sonograms, a certain obstetrician appeared to be 100 percent accurate in predicting the gender of his deliveries. Shortly before the due date, the doctor told the expectant mother that the baby was the gender she hoped for. Under the guise of protecting their recollections, the physician scribbled a word and placed the note in his file. What the new mother did not know was the doctor wrote on the slip of paper the opposite gender from what she was hoping for. If the new arrival was the sex the mother preferred, the doctor gloated. If the infant was opposite from what he predicted, the doctor would say, "Let's look in the file and see what I wrote down. Here it is. Your baby is the sex I wrote down!"

Paul had some explaining to do about his on-again, off-again visits.

Paul's critics leveled their allegations against him on two counts. First, he was undependable, and second, he made plans on his own without the leadership of the Holy Spirit. It was unthinkable! He recognized how those accusations could undermine his entire ministry and place all of his work in jeopardy. If he were unreliable, his message was unreliable. If the Holy Spirit did not lead him, then Paul's message was not Spirit-led. It was imperative that the Corinthians see Paul as totally trustworthy so they would not discount his message.

Paul countered their claims by declaring that his word could be depended on. His position was as steadfast as the Lord Jesus himself. All of God's prophecies and promises had waited to be confirmed. Then Jesus came. Jesus was God's emphatic affirmation of each and every one of them. The truth of God's every promise was fulfilled in Christ. He was God's confirmation, God's resounding "Amen."

> *The truth of God's every promise was fulfilled in Christ.*

In synagogues and homes, it was customary for the people present to affirm audibly the prayers that were offered (1 Corinthians 14:16). Not only public prayers but private prayers and doxologies were appropriately concluded with "amen" (Romans 9:5; 11:36). The term "amen" is variously translated *so be it, true,* or *that which is true.* "Amen" was the stamp of truth on an assertion that made it as binding as an oath (see Deuteronomy 27:14–26).

Paul explained that Christ proved God's absolute veracity. Jesus was God's "Yes" to all God's past Messianic promises and all God pledged in the future (2 Cor. 1:20). Paul equated his stability to God's stability. Paul

Church Discipline

Corrective discipline is a scriptural responsibility of the church (Matthew 18:15–17). It functions to protect the purity and unity of the congregation. God's glory is at stake, and conduct that reflects negatively on the church is a legitimate cause for discipline. Actions such as serious contentions between members, immorality, disorderly behavior, or erroneous teaching may be subject to discipline. It should apply to all church members. Ideally, it will work to the spiritual good of both the offender(s) and the fellowship

Church discipline should be practiced as a last resort, after all other measures have failed. The congregation needs to agree disciplinary action is necessary. The Matthew passage offers specific instruction on the steps to follow. The by-laws of every church should specify the procedure for handling discipline. Its severest form, exclusion from fellowship, may be necessary (see Titus 3:10–11).

Loving church discipline needs to accomplish at least three goals: allow repentance and restoration for the offender(s); provide a solution for the church; and show the unbelieving world the holiness of Christ's body, the church.

was not haphazard in either his planning or his ministry. He sought and followed the Lord's leading.

The issue of Paul's character was a serious matter. He saw it as fundamental to his ministry. He was confident in his innocence. To strengthen his testimony, he appealed to God to be his witness (1:23). It was no casual request. God was sometimes called to be a witness because God not only was present and knew all the circumstances, but also God's character as a righteous judge vouched for the integrity of the person on trial (Job 16:19–21; Psalm 89:34–37). By placing himself before God in such a way, Paul was virtually asking God to take his life if he were lying.

Paul saw five ways God was at work in the fellowship, as follows:

First, Christ empowered them to be steadfast (1:21). Christ's power may be one of the most frequently overlooked resources available to us as Christians. Through Jesus, we have the power available to handle every situation, resist every temptation, and overcome every condition in life. Paul described the magnitude of Christ's power when he wrote, "I can do everything through him who gives me strength" (Philippians 4:13). We sometimes think of death as being the ultimate power, but God's power is even greater. His power raised Jesus from the grave. Too, God's amazing power is available to us! Paul implied that believers had the power to resist the temptation to abandon his teaching and to remain steadfast in the things he taught them.

> *Christ's power may be one of the most frequently overlooked resources available to us as Christians.*

Second, they had been "anointed" (meaning consecrated) for service (1:21). Anointing was an important religious ritual throughout the Bible. It was a social duty, as with a host anointing the head of his guest (Luke 7:46). It was a medical treatment for the sick (James 5:14). It was a solemn rite used to consecrate articles and people (1 Samuel 10:1). In the Old Testament, priests and kings were anointed with a special preparation of oil to signify their appointment by God for service. The ceremony represented their being set part for God's purposes. Paul considered the Corinthian Christians to be likewise set apart for service.

Third, God placed his "seal of ownership" on them (1:22). Seals were important in Eastern culture; they were required on all legal documents. In their various forms, they were used in several ways to prevent anyone from tampering with the contents. In sealing an official document, a tomb, or a box, the closure was covered with clay or wax and stamped with the seal of the one who held authority over it. Paul explained that the Corinthians carried God's mark of ownership, the seal of the Holy Spirit.

Fourth, God sent the Holy Spirit to indwell their hearts (1:22). The Holy Spirit was in the world from the beginning of creation, but after Pentecost, the Holy Spirit came to live in all believers (Acts 2:1–4).

Fifth, the presence of the Holy Spirit in their lives ensured their future with God (1:23). Paul explained that the presence of the Holy Spirit in their lives guaranteed they were saved and would receive much more when Christ returned. What they were experiencing of the Holy Spirit was only a sampling of the benefits of their future inheritance. The Holy Spirit was like a down payment on a purchase.

> . . . *God's amazing power is available to us!*

In verse 24, Paul's clear definition of roles may have been in response to an accusation that he was infringing on their freedom in Christ. He insisted he had no intention of exercising ecclesiastical control over them. Paul would never try to usurp the Lord's role. He was just glad his role was to help them develop spiritually, attain the joy of their salvation, and mature in their faith. He pointed out that their steadfastness was related to their faith.

Still trying to make the case for his itinerary change, Paul tried to explain the basis for his decision. Apparently his most recent visit was mutually painful, a grief to both him and the church. If everyone were grief-stricken, he reasoned, there would be no one to offer comfort. So instead of visiting as he had said he would, he wrote a letter (see 7:8).

Paul hoped the letter would win over the offenders. The letter was difficult to write. Paul wrote under duress. Perhaps as he wrote, their faces one by one came to mind, people he loved and likely many of whom he had won to the Lord. Each convert was important to him and a personal joy as he saw them maturing in their faith. Rebuking the Corinthians broke Paul's heart. He was anguished and tearful (2:4).

Restoring Relationships (2:5–11)

Next Paul dealt with church discipline. In his painful letter, he had insisted the church must not let a troublemaker go unpunished. It is unclear what the trouble was. Biblical scholars offer several possible explanations. A

Case Study

Bert and his family were new members in the church. Bert joined the choir. He had a beautiful, trained voice. He became the featured soloist for the church's weekly radio program. After a few Sundays, a merchant called the church and reported that Bert had bad credit in the community. How do you suggest the situation be handled?

common view is that an individual had challenged Paul's authority and convinced others to abandon his teaching.

Paul insisted the offending person had to be disciplined. Otherwise, Satan would seize the situation, and the man would continue to keep the church in turmoil and destroy their unity. The recommended action was what we sometimes call *tough love*. The action was to be firm, loving, and forgiving. The goal was restoration, not excommunication. Paul saw their decision as a test of loyalty to him. The majority followed Paul's suggestion, and the man repented. Once the man repented, Paul admonished the Corinthians to follow his example and forgive the offender. They were to renew their relationship with him and work toward harmony. If they continued to be harsh, he reasoned, the offender might withdraw, return to his old ways, and thereby give Satan another advantage. It was time to heal the breach.

> *Like Paul, we can be forthright yet forgiving when dealing with strained relationships.*

During my early years my grandparents attended the church I attend now. I had known that my grandfather was smitten with my grandmother when they were young and attending a small rural church. But I learned some astonishing information after they died. A woman came to my door with the early church minutes under her arm. "I want you to see something," she said, as she opened the tattered book. There it was! My grandfather had been *churched* until he *changed his ways*. What was his terrible sin? Chewing tobacco! The discipline worked. My grandfather continued to attend church and never used tobacco in any form the rest of his life.

Implications for Today

Like Paul, we can be forthright yet forgiving when dealing with strained relationships. We can find ways to be kind and loving.

QUESTIONS

1. How do you think Christian history would be different if Paul had not been converted?

2. How is the Holy Spirit evident in your church? in your life?

3. How is church discipline practiced in your church?

4. What actions of Paul in dealing with the strained relationships with the Corinthians would be helpful in a situation of which you are aware?

Background

2 Corinthians 2:14—3:18

Main Idea

Christian ministry should be measured by Christian standards.

Question to Explore

How can ministry be measured?

Study Aim

To identify the ways in which Paul measured his ministry and evaluate my ministry and my church's ministry in light of them

Study and Action Emphases

- Affirm the Bible as our authoritative guide for life and ministry
- Share the gospel with all people
- Develop a growing, vibrant faith
- Include all God's family in decision-making and service
- Value all people as created in the image of God
- Equip people for servant leadership

LESSON THREE

Measuring Our Ministry

Quick Read

Paul thanked God for his ministry and gave God the credit.

How do you measure success? Different professions require different standards. When electricians flip a switch and the light comes on, they can assume they did a good job. When plumbers turn the water on and the pipes don't leak, they can be sure they connected the pipes correctly. When an artist paints a picture that is acclaimed by his or her peers or when a musician receives a standing ovation, they are termed "successful." But how do we determine the success of someone's ministry? We do well to consider Paul's method of evaluation.

Paul was distraught over the effect his "painful letter" might have had on the Corinthian Christians. In it, likely he chided them for questioning his apostolic calling and his ministry. Titus, a Greek (Gentile) emissary whom Paul dispatched to Corinth to deliver the letter, brought back some good news (2 Corinthians 7:5–7). Many of the church members received Paul's message well, repented of their departure from his teachings and renewed their spiritual allegiance to him. Paul was exuberant even though there was still a rebel faction.

Greatly relieved that the believers understood and were following his admonitions, Paul burst into a crescendo of praise. His use of "us" and "we" may have been editorial usage, referring to himself in the plural, or he might have been including Timothy. Too, he might have been including the Corinthians in the "us" and "we."

The miracle of God's transforming power that turned Paul, a hard-hearted Pharisee, into a loving, caring Christian, had convicted the Corinthians and changed their hearts. His relationship with them was restored! It was a marvelous work, and he gave all credit to God. Suddenly, Paul glimpsed a panoramic view of the way God had used him to bring so many people to Christ. He remembered other situations in which God had triumphed. Although Paul had suffered frequently, God never failed him, and people came to know Christ as a result. Paul used a familiar analogy to describe God's glorious pursuits.

2 Corinthians 2:14—3:6

[14]But thanks be to God, who always leads us in triumphal procession in Christ and through us spreads everywhere the fragrance of the knowledge of him. [15]For we are to God the aroma of Christ among those who are being saved and those who are perishing. [16]To the one we are the smell of death; to the other, the fragrance of life. And who is equal to such a task?

> [17]Unlike so many, we do not peddle the word of God for profit. On the contrary, in Christ we speak before God with sincerity, like men sent from God.
>
> [3:1]Are we beginning to commend ourselves again? Or do we need, like some people, letters of recommendation to you or from you? [2]You yourselves are our letter, written on our hearts, known and read by everybody. [3]You show that you are a letter from Christ, the result of our ministry, written not with ink but with the Spirit of the living God, not on tablets of stone but on tablets of human hearts.
>
> [4]Such confidence as this is ours through Christ before God. [5]Not that we are competent in ourselves to claim anything for ourselves, but our competence comes from God. [6]He has made us competent as ministers of a new covenant—not of the letter but of the Spirit; for the letter kills, but the Spirit gives life.

Christ's "Triumph" (2:14–16)

When a victorious Roman general returned from combat, he participated in a huge parade called a "triumph." He entered the city of Rome and proceeded down the *Via Sacre* (Sacred Way). The participants paraded through the throng-filled street. The crowd shouted and cheered as the procession passed by. The celebration was extravagant, the highest honor awarded to a conquering commander. It might happen only once in a lifetime. The celebration ended with sacrificial offerings and a public feast.

Although Paul had suffered frequently, God never failed him, and people came to know Christ as a result.

That is the picture Paul had in mind when he remembered how Christ always triumphed over his enemies. He saw Christ as the conquering hero, marching throughout the world. Perhaps Paul saw himself not as one of the honored officers riding beside the general but first as one of the miserable hostages. Then he saw himself as one of the incense bearers strewing the fragrance of Christ wherever he went. The aroma of Christ that filled the air Paul likened to the sweet smell of victory in the conquerors' nostrils but the stench of death to the prisoners.

Paul thought he and his colleagues were highly privileged to preach the gospel of the triumphant Christ. Just as the smell of the incense filled the air and could not be confined, the good news they preached could not be restrained. The aroma of Christ permeated the spiritual atmosphere wherever the gospel was shared.

When Paul considered the magnitude of his call, he was awestruck. No mere human being could produce such amazing results, certainly not he and not the false teachers who peddled religion among the Corinthians. The word Paul used for "peddle" carried the idea of being a huckster who tricked people into purchasing an inferior product.

Living Letters (3:1–6)

Paul again introduced the subject of letters of recommendation. The scalawags who had come to Corinth to undermine his character and undo his work may have been Jewish sympathizers. They were armed with letters recommending themselves. They criticized Paul because he had none.

Who can estimate the power of a letter? When my friend moved to another state to accept a church staff position, she left her trunk with me. It remained unopened until her sudden death in a car accident. In time, I opened it and found an open letter addressed to her father, who was not a Christian. She pleaded with him to accept Christ as his Savior. I promptly sent the letter to him. Several months later, he repented, made his profession of faith in Christ, and was baptized into the fellowship of the church that had also prayed and witnessed to him for years.

How do you measure success?

On second thought, if it were letters the skeptics wanted, Paul had them. They were living, breathing, and moving around. They were the Corinthian believers! Actually, Paul had numerous "letters" since each Christian was a letter from Christ written by the life-giving Spirit, not inscribed by human beings with ink that could fade or be washed away. They were a permanent record for everyone to read. After all, most of them were relatively new in the faith, and yet their transformation was astonishing (1 Corinthians 6:9–11). Their lives were indisputable proof that Paul's work was valid.

Their changed lives also affirmed Paul's confidence concerning his divine appointment. Yet he refused to claim any credit for the content of the gospel or its effects. Unlike the tablets of stone that held the Ten Commandments (Deuteronomy 5:1–22), the Holy Spirit used the gospel

Old and New Covenants

A biblical covenant refers to a binding agreement initiated by God to bring God's people into right relationship with himself. He sets the terms to be fulfilled. God made a covenant with Abraham and his descendants (Genesis 17:4–7). God continued this covenant through Moses and the Ten Commandments (Exodus 20:1–17; Deuteronomy 5:1–21). The stones on which God engraved the Ten Commandments were called "the tablets of the covenant" (Deut. 9:11).

The shed blood of Christ inaugurated the new covenant (Matthew 26:28; Luke 22:20; 1 Corinthians 11:25). The old covenant required continual sacrifices for sin, but Jesus' death provided the perfect, final sacrifice. It brings about a spiritual change in a person that alters his or her nature, enabling a person to respond to God in faith. This change is based on grace and forgiveness (Ephesians 2:1–5).

Paul preached to inscribe the new covenant on the hearts of believers—hearts that were softened by grace. No external message could produce the divine action necessary to reach the deep recesses within the hearts of unbelievers (Jeremiah 31:33; Ezekiel 36:26).

The Two Covenants (3:7–18)

Paul next compared Moses' ministry and his own ministry in relationship to the two covenants—the Old and the New. Much of biblical theology is founded on the covenant relationship between God and God's people. This covenant relationship goes back to the beginning of Israelite tradition. God always initiated the covenants and specified the requirements for the people to meet. The Ten Commandments prescribed the basic religious and moral ideals that set Israel apart as a holy nation. The Ten Commandments came to represent the old covenant, the law.

Paul associated Moses' ministry of the law with personal effort—an endless, necessary duty. Even though Moses' ministry held a splendor that was reflected in Moses' face after his communion with God (Exodus 34:29–30), it was a fleeting glory. Moses wore a veil to conceal the fading radiance. Paul said

The miracle of God's transforming power that turned Paul, a hard-hearted Pharisee, into a loving, caring Christian, had convicted the Corinthians and changed their hearts.

Church Rivalry

The rivalry between the churches was legendary. Both pastors enjoyed the friendly competition. Year after year they challenged each other with higher and higher goals in Sunday School attendance. Sometimes the auditoriums were encircled with cute little cutouts posted on the walls. Each motif represented a person's pledge to attend regularly for the specified period of time. Both churches grew and grew. What are the positives and negatives of using gimmicks and/or rivalry to measure the ministry of pastors and churches?

---

the transient nature of Moses' glory pointed to the impermanence of the law. Paul contended the old covenant (law) demanded an unobtainable standard. Its effect was external. It could only condemn. It exposed the sinfulness of people and the accompanying wrath of God. It pronounced a death sentence on humanity. As a zealous Pharisee, Paul knew first hand about the law's impossible requirements and the constant effort it demanded.

For medical reasons my brother's driver's license was suspended until he recovered from a critical illness. He had to overcome the effects of his illness, his medicine, and his physical limitations. The test to reinstate his license had several parts. Some parts could be taken in the office with specialized equipment; the other parts required him actually to drive his car. All of it was based on state laws.

> *Paul thought he and his colleagues were highly privileged to preach the gospel of the triumphant Christ.*

My brother passed the simulator operation and written parts with flying colors, but he failed the vision test. The woman in charge was patient and sympathetic, but my brother's eyesight was impaired. She had no power to correct his problem or change the requirements. Since neither he nor she could "fix" my brother's eyes, the vision test just revealed his inadequacy. That is the way the old covenant operated. While it showed the standard God required, it pronounced universal failure. It could never justify. It could only condemn. It could never free. It was, in a sense, lethal.

Paul was captivated by the new covenant Christ inaugurated at the conclusion of the Last Supper (Luke 22:20). It had an inner power and vitality. Its superiority was based on the work of the Holy Spirit in hearts, not on stone. Christ fulfilled the law and died, taking God's wrath upon himself (2 Corinthians 5:19; Galatians 3:13; Colossians 2:14). He freed those

38

who received him from constantly trying to gain God's favor by obeying the law. The gospel now provides for the law's fulfillment through the power of the Risen Christ (Romans 10:4).

The new covenant necessitated ministers qualified by the Holy Spirit (1 Timothy 1:12). The apostolic preachers knew God's final word to humankind was Jesus (Hebrews 1:1–2). That and other great certainties of the gospel gave Christian preachers a unique ministry. They were ministers not only of the written word, the law, but also, by the gospel, they ministered both the word and the Spirit.

Who can estimate the power of a letter?

Rather than the glory being limited to one person—Moses—God's glory rests in every believer through the indwelling Christ. That glory does not fade or diminish. Instead, it increases by degrees, from glory to glory, as Christ's followers come to experience more and more of him.

Implications for Today

To measure Paul's success in ministry, as well as our own and our church's, we need to look at his method, which was sincere (2:17–18); his purpose, which was to help people become Christ-like (3:1–3); and his authority, which was total reliance on God (3:5). Should we not measure our church's ministry—and ours—by these same standards?

QUESTIONS

1. Refer to 2 Corinthians 2:14–16. In the picture of Christ's "triumph," (victorious procession), what group would you be in? Why?

2. What does it mean that Christians are letters, "known and read by everybody" (2 Cor. 2:2)?

3. What does Paul's idea of the Corinthian Christians as being "a letter from Christ, the result of our ministry" (2:3) suggest about measuring Christian ministry?

4. What are your standards for measuring ministry? How do they compare to Paul's?

Focal Text

2 Corinthians 4:1–15

Background

2 Corinthians 4:1–15

Main Idea

Maintaining heart for the work of ministry in the face of challenges calls for wholehearted faithfulness to and trust in God.

Question to Explore

How can we keep from becoming discouraged in Christian service?

Study Aim

To identify elements in how Paul maintained heart for Christian ministry that we need to practice

Study and Action Emphases

- Affirm the Bible as our authoritative guide for life and ministry
- Share the gospel with all people
- Develop a growing, vibrant faith
- Obey and serve Jesus by meeting physical, spiritual, and emotional needs
- Equip people for servant leadership

LESSON FOUR

Maintaining Heart for Ministry

Quick Read

God's power overcame human weakness and empowered Paul for ministry so that he did not despair when troubles came.

My grandson, James, is majoring in electrical engineering in college. He called one day with a message that cheered my heart. "Grammy," he said, "I want to thank you for the times you wouldn't let me stop when things didn't work out the first time I tried. I think that is why I have done so well developing my projects now. I just keep working until I finally succeed."

In his formative years, James enjoyed helping me with "projects," but he tended to be impatient. He got frustrated and wanted to quit when our first efforts failed. I insisted we return to the task and keep working until we accomplished our goal. Giving up was not an option.

Discouragement seems to be a universal temptation. Throughout this chapter, Paul used the plural pronoun "we." He could be referring to his fellow ministers, or perhaps he was including the Corinthian believers. A third possibility is that he used the term as the editorial "we." Nevertheless, careful study reveals at least ten reasons to "not lose heart" (2 Corinthians 4:1). These reasons are couched in language that is sometimes difficult to unravel, but the insights are there. Watch for them and compare your findings with my suggestions. (Notice the numbers in parentheses.) We would do well to emulate them.

2 Corinthians 4:1–15

[1]Therefore, since through God's mercy we have this ministry, we do not lose heart. [2]Rather, we have renounced secret and shameful ways; we do not use deception, nor do we distort the word of God. On the contrary, by setting forth the truth plainly we commend ourselves to every man's conscience in the sight of God. [3]And even if our gospel is veiled, it is veiled to those who are perishing. [4]The god of this age has blinded the minds of unbelievers, so that they cannot see the light of the gospel of the glory of Christ, who is the image of God. [5]For we do not preach ourselves, but Jesus Christ as Lord, and ourselves as your servants for Jesus' sake. [6]For God, who said, "Let light shine out of darkness," made his light shine in our hearts to give us the light of the knowledge of the glory of God in the face of Christ.

[7]But we have this treasure in jars of clay to show that this all-surpassing power is from God and not from us. [8]We are hard pressed on every side, but not crushed; perplexed, but not in despair; [9]persecuted, but not abandoned; struck down, but not destroyed. [10]We always carry around in our body the death of Jesus, so that the life of Jesus may also be revealed in our body. [11]For we who are alive are always being given over to death

for Jesus' sake, so that his life may be revealed in our mortal body. [12]So then, death is at work in us, but life is at work in you.

[13]It is written: "I believed; therefore I have spoken." With that same spirit of faith we also believe and therefore speak, [14]because we know that the one who raised the Lord Jesus from the dead will also raise us with Jesus and present us with you in his presence. [15]All this is for your benefit, so that the grace that is reaching more and more people may cause thanksgiving to overflow to the glory of God.

Paul Finds Encouragement (4:1–6)

(#1) The sheer wonder of God's mercy and grace whereby God saved, called, and commissioned his people to service, in Paul's case to evangelize the Gentiles, was ever present in Paul's thinking (4:1). Not by Paul's choice or merit did he become a minister of the gospel. He was "less than the least of all God's people" (Ephesians 3:8) and "the worst" of sinners (1 Timothy 1:15). Then God apprehended him and changed his purpose from violence, hatred, and death to love, reconciliation, and service. Yet nothing about his previous life was wasted. His education at the feet of the renowned Hebrew teacher, Gamaliel (Acts 22:3), his Roman citizenship (Acts 22:25–28), and even his fanatical religious background made him a better servant. The miraculous nature of his personal experience with the Living Lord was like a spiritual fountain that constantly refreshed his soul.

(#2) Paul was encouraged by the truth of the gospel (2 Cor. 4:2). Jesus said, "I am the way and the truth and the life. No one comes to the Father except through me" (John 14:6). The truth did not need to be camouflaged or embellished. It needed only to be proclaimed. It was centered in a person—Jesus. Without sham or shame, Paul simply preached Christ's life, death, and resurrection. He never soft-pedaled the need for repentance, the cost of discipleship, and the Lordship of Christ. Jesus promised "the truth will set you free" (John 8:32), and Paul's compelling purpose in presenting the gospel was to set people free from bondage.

(#3) Paul took heart because the gospel was valid whether people believed it or not (2 Cor. 4:3–4). Their decision to reject the gospel had no effect on the message. Although Satan could blind the hearts of some, the gospel was still trustworthy. "The god of this age" only gained his way with individuals because they chose to yield to him.

Any temptation to discouragement was quickly banished when Paul considered the results of his ministry (4:5). He appealed to people's spiritual hunger, not merely to their intellect or emotions. He never tried to manipulate anyone. His message was intended for those who had a genuine desire to know God. To those who were open to it, his message was understandable and welcomed. But to those who chose not to believe, his message was concealed, hidden behind a veil. Unlike the false teachers who resorted to distortion and deception, Paul was careful to present the gospel in clear, sincere, and straightforward terms.

Dr. Billy Graham, the famous evangelist, has known some of the most prestigious people in the world. He has many celebrities among his friends and acquaintances. He has met with presidents, royalty, and other heads of state. Since 1949, he has preached in the United States, England, Scotland, the Soviet Union, the Middle East, the Far East, South America, and Africa. His radio program, "The Hour of Decision," has aired for more than fifty years. He has appeared on television and written several successful books. Two of his children have worldwide ministries also. Yet Dr. Graham remains an humble servant of the Lord. He has never wavered from his original clear and simple terminology that emphasizes God's love, repentance, and the plan of salvation in Christ.

Discouragement seems to be a universal temptation.

(#4) The force of the gospel encouraged Paul (4:6). He likened it to God's first recorded creative act when God said, "'Let there be light,' and there was light" (Genesis 1:3). Out of chaotic darkness the light of God's glory appeared. Then, in an orderly fashion, God proceeded with creation. Similarly, Paul encountered the force of Christ's light on the Damascus road. The brilliance that blinded his eyes penetrated and enlightened his dark and tormented soul. Although God did marvelous works through Paul, Paul never took credit for himself. He was honored that his "claim to fame" was being a Christ-appointed servant to the Corinthians.

Treasures Hidden in Unexpected Places (4:7)

Many gadget catalogues advertise products designed to conceal valuables. You can hide your door key in an artificial rock and place it in your flower bed. You can install a wall safe behind a beautiful picture. Or, you can store your treasures in a mock electrical switch.

When a friend remodeled her home, the carpenter thought he was doing her a favor when he created a super-hiding place for whatever she wanted to protect. It was a hollow bin under the bottom shelf of her bookcase. She never used it. It was too much trouble to unload and reload the books when she wanted to store or retrieve her valuables.

Unlike the false teachers who resorted to distortion and deception, Paul was careful to present the gospel in clear, sincere, and straightforward terms.

(**#5**) Paul was encouraged that God would put his mighty power in weak humanity such as himself and the Corinthians. It was like a treasure deposited in a common clay jar. In Paul's day, pottery lamps were a necessity in every household. They were available in the markets for a nominal charge. It did not matter that the container was cheap or fragile. The value of the vessel was not in its workmanship but in its contents. It held the wick and the oil that illuminated its surroundings.

Paul likely was no tall, dark, and handsome model of a man. He was probably small, bald-headed, and bowlegged, with a rugged, scarred physique. He suffered some malady that was debilitating at times. He called it "a thorn in the flesh" (12:7). His appearance left much to be desired (10:10). No one would suspect a priceless treasure was housed in such an unimposing person. The real treasure was the power that resided within the gospel message Paul was privileged to share.

Treasure in Clay Jars

Making pottery was one of the oldest crafts in Bible lands. The potter mixed clay with water and then fashioned various utensils. The potter fired the pieces in an open flame or a kiln, a high-heat oven. Most household utensils were made this way. Unlike other artifacts, pottery can survive for thousands of years.

In 1947, herdsmen made one of the greatest discoveries related to the Bible since the early centuries of Christianity. They found hundreds of ancient scrolls and scroll fragments hidden in eleven caves at Qumran, near the Dead Sea. Many of the scrolls were biblical manuscripts. Portions of almost every book of the Old Testament were found.

Some of the manuscripts are said to be more than 1,000 years older than any other Old Testament manuscripts known to exist. The documents, called the Dead Sea Scrolls, are believed to be the library of a Jewish sect that lived just before and during the time of Jesus.

How was this treasure preserved for centuries? In common clay jars!

God's Abundant Resources (4:8–14)

(#6) God's limitless and readily available resources constantly encouraged Paul (4:8–9). He saw them in a series of paradoxes. He might be afflicted, but he was never destroyed; perplexed but not despairing; persecuted by people but never forsaken by God; knocked down but never knocked out. Seemingly when he came to the end of his rope, he always found hope.

Hope is a recurring theme in both the Old and the New Testaments. It is the expectation of something good to come about. It means the pres-

Without sham or shame, Paul simply preached Christ's life, death, and resurrection.

ence of a future. Jeremiah expressed this idea when he wrote, "For I know the plans I have for you . . . plans to prosper you and not to harm you, plans to give you a hope and a future" (Jeremiah 29:11). What encouragement! We can hope because God knows our future and God's plans for us are good. This does not mean we will never experience pain, disappointment, and all kinds of difficulties. We can, however, anticipate God's presence with us, God's help as we deal with our circumstances, and God's faithfulness that will see us through to a glorious end.

Christian hope is often connected with the return of Jesus Christ at the end of this age and the resurrection of the dead (1 Thessalonians 1:10; Acts 1:11; Titus 2:13). Christian hope gives purpose and meaning to life. Hope is the "God factor" in every situation. But hope must have a secure resting place. Otherwise we are doomed to futility, disappointment, and depression. The Old Testament writers testified that God alone offered the secure foundation hope needed. The Israelites learned patience and courage as they looked and waited for their hope to be fulfilled.

In the New Testament, the focus changes from confident expectation to the reality of the indwelling Christ who, according to Paul, is "in you, the hope of glory" (Colossians 1:27). Paul's hope was rooted in Christ's resurrection and victory over death. Thus he associated hope in Christ with confidence (Romans 4:18; Philippians 1:6), rejoicing (Rom. 5:2), endurance (Rom. 5:4), freedom (Rom. 8:20–21), and love (1 Cor. 13:7). New Testament hope is personal and corporate. It is perceived as both a present reality and a future expectation. The Book of Revelation is a book of hope. It shows that no matter what happens on earth (or in our lives), God is in control.

Danger and the threat of death were Paul's constant companions (2 Cor. 4:10–12). His sufferings began immediately after his conversion and continued in unbroken succession for more than thirty years. There were plots to kill him in Damascus (Acts 9:24) and in Jerusalem (Acts 9:29). He was driven out of Antioch in Pisidia (Acts 13:50). His enemies attempted to stone him in Iconium (Acts 14:1–5). They did stone him in Lystra, leaving him for dead (Acts 14:19). In Philippi he was beaten with rods and put in stocks (Acts 16:23–24). The Jews tried to mob him (Acts 17:5) in Thessalonica. He was driven out of Berea (Acts 17:13–14). There were plots against him in Corinth (Acts 18:12), and he was almost killed in Ephesus (2 Cor.1:8–9).

Paul's compelling purpose in presenting the gospel was to set people free from bondage.

Shortly after he wrote 2 Corinthians, his life was again in danger (Acts 20:3). Later in Jerusalem, he would have been killed had it not been for the Roman soldiers (Acts 22:22–24). He was imprisoned in Caesarea for two years and for two more years in Rome. There were other recorded and unrecorded beatings, imprisonments, shipwrecks, and strenuous privations of every kind (2 Cor. 11:23–27). Finally, he was taken to Rome in chains to be tried (2 Timothy 2:9). These persecutions took their toll on Paul's body and emotions, but not on his spirit. As his body grew more and more infirm, people could see more and more of the Lord Jesus.

How did he do it? How did Paul continue to persevere in the face of such ominous happenings? **(#7)** He discovered the secret of daily renewal that Jeremiah wrote about in Lamentations 3:21–23. "Yet this I call to mind and therefore I have hope: because of the Lord's great love we are not consumed, for his compassions never fail, they are new every morning: great is your faithfulness." (See 2 Cor. 4:11, "always.")

(#8) Paul's unshakable faith sustained him in trying times (4:13). He never doubted God's ability or availability. As God had demonstrated his power and trustworthiness in the past, Paul was confident God could be trusted in the present and the future.

(#9) Eternal life was a reality in Paul's thinking. That cheered his heart and kept him from being downcast (4:14). His constant exposure to the threats posed by his enemies forced him to come to terms with death. No matter how dire Paul's circumstances were, he had a knack for evaluating them in the light of eternity. He saw the here and now as a temporary state when compared to eternity. He considered the invisible rewards of heaven more important than the trials on earth. As a Pharisee, Paul believed in the resurrection as a possibility; as a Christian, Paul knew it as a certainty.

The Scope of Paul's Ministry (4:15)

(#10) Paul was heartened by the ever-expanding boundaries of his ministry. His first efforts to share Christ were in the synagogues of Damascus shortly after his conversion (Acts 9:19–22). He preached what he knew: Jesus is the Son of God. From that seemingly meager beginning in Damascus, he became Christianity's foremost missionary.

We can hope because God knows our future and God's plans for us are good.

A quick glance at a map showing Paul's journeys reveals he was always on the forefront of spreading the gospel. Each journey took him to new frontiers. He planted churches in Galatia, Asia, Macedonia, and Achaia. He was always challenged by the unevangelized world that was just beyond his present ministry. He selected and trained strong Christians to help him and to continue the Lord's work after his death.

Implications for Today

In his letter to the Galatians, Paul cited yet another reason for not growing weary and giving up. A harvest is waiting for those who persevere (Gal. 6:9).

Case Study

Following the church service one Sunday, Faye and Helen were discussing the sermon. When they asked their friend what she thought about the message, she said, "I don't remember a word of it. I go to church because I feel I ought to, but I sit there and think about other things. I'm really not interested in the sermon." What could Faye and Helen do to help their friend open her heart to God's message?

QUESTIONS

1. Why did Paul continue to teach and preach in spite of persecution?

2. What sources of encouragement would you add to the items identified in this lesson?

3. How would the spread of Christianity have been different if Paul had given up?

Focal Text

2 Corinthians 4:16—5:10

Background

2 Corinthians 4:16—5:10

Main Idea

Through God's power and guaranteed by the Spirit's presence, we can face the difficulties of life and even death with confidence.

Question to Explore

When life tumbles in and death must be faced, what hope is there?

Study Aim

To affirm with confidence the assurance God offers for facing the difficulties of life and even death

Study and Action Emphases

- Affirm the Bible as our authoritative guide for life and ministry
- Develop a growing, vibrant faith

LESSON FIVE

Confidence for Now and Forever

Quick Read

Although believers cannot reverse the effects of aging and death, they can live positively and minister effectively while looking forward to a home in heaven.

One of the most dynamic Christians I have ever met was a senior adult named David Bush. He was a faithful member of the church I served as pastor. He attended Bible study and sang in the worship choir. He became so crippled he could hardly walk, but he continued to participate fully in the life of the church. He never complained that because of his many physical problems it took him longer to do things than most people.

Finally, a day came when David could no longer attend church. He was confined to a care home in the city. Every time I visited him in the care home, I was met with a vibrant smile and a positive comment. All those who worked at the care home talked about David's personal encouragement to them. He shared his faith in Jesus with everyone he met.

One day David said to me, "Preacher, I don't know why God leaves me here. There must be one more person who needs to hear about Jesus." Even though David looked forward to his release from crippling illness and to his home in heaven, he wanted every day he had left on earth to be one that was pleasing to God.

As we study this part of Paul's second Corinthian letter, we can learn that through the power of the Holy Spirit we can remain positive and productive in the midst of aging and death.

2 Corinthians 4:16—5:10

[16]Therefore we do not lose heart. Though outwardly we are wasting away, yet inwardly we are being renewed day by day. [17]For our light and momentary troubles are achieving for us an eternal glory that far outweighs them all. [18]So we fix our eyes not on what is seen, but on what is unseen. For what is seen is temporary, but what is unseen is eternal.

[5:1]Now we know that if the earthly tent we live in is destroyed, we have a building from God, an eternal house in heaven, not built by human hands. [2]Meanwhile we groan, longing to be clothed with our heavenly dwelling, [3]because when we are clothed, we will not be found naked. [4]For while we are in this tent, we groan and are burdened, because we do not wish to be unclothed but to be clothed with our heavenly dwelling, so that what is mortal may be swallowed up by life. [5]Now it is God who has made us for this very purpose and has given us the Spirit as a deposit, guaranteeing what is to come.

[6]Therefore we are always confident and know that as long as we are at home in the body we are away from the Lord. [7]We live by faith, not by sight. [8]We are confident, I say, and would prefer to be away from the body and at home with the Lord. [9]So we make it our goal to please him,

> whether we are at home in the body or away from it. [10] For we must all appear before the judgment seat of Christ, that each one may receive what is due him for the things done while in the body, whether good or bad.

Growing Stronger While Growing Weaker (4:16–18)

Paul introduced this part of his letter with the word, "therefore." The word refers us back to his discussion in 4:1–15 about the struggles every believer faces in this life. Even with these struggles, Paul wrote that the believer does not "lose heart" (4:1, 16).

What does it mean to "lose heart"? It means to lose courage. What would have caused Paul's readers to "lose heart"? The two things mentioned immediately are "wasting away" and "our light and momentary troubles" (4:17).

Every adult knows what it means to "waste away." It means to grow older and weaker. Even though the average lifespan is getting longer, the mortality rate is still 100 percent. I'm reminded of one ninety-eight-year-old woman who was asked what she liked most about being ninety-eight. She replied, "No peer pressure." Then she added, "No peers."

This "wasting away" comes naturally with age, but it can be hastened by the kinds of problems Paul was facing. He was being "hard pressed" (4:8), "persecuted" (4:9), and "struck down" (4:9).

Even though David looked forward to his release from crippling illness and to his home in heaven, he wanted every day he had left on earth to be one that was pleasing to God.

He described these troubles as "light and momentary" compared to what they were achieving in his life—a glory that is more valuable than any trouble. The author of Hebrews wrote that Jesus "for the joy set before him endured the cross" (Hebrews 12:2). Jesus never spoke to his disciples about his death without also speaking about his resurrection. His death was accomplishing something more valuable than pain and suffering. It was accomplishing our salvation.

Troubles can either beat us down or fire us up. Sometimes problems that cause the body to age or grow weaker actually cause the spirit to grow stronger. Paul was "outwardly . . . wasting away" but "inwardly . . . being renewed day by day" (2 Cor. 4:16).

It is significant that Paul wrote that believers are "being renewed." Believers don't have the power to renew themselves. Something or someone is renewing the believer even as he or she is "wasting away." This someone is Jesus Christ through the power of the Holy Spirit.

Paul reminded the Corinthian believers that even though they were nothing more than "jars of clay" (4:8), they had a treasure within powered by God himself. This power within kept them from being "destroyed" (4:9). Paul described his personal experience with this power shown in God's care (4:7–11) and God's promise to raise him also with Jesus (4:14).

Even though the average lifespan is getting longer, the mortality rate is still 100 percent.

The believer grows stronger while growing weaker by having a different vision of life and death. Paul wrote that we "fix our eyes . . . on what is unseen" (4:18). The writer of Hebrews credited Moses' success as a leader to this kind of vision, "he persevered because he saw him who is invisible" (Hebrews 11:27).

To grow younger while growing older, one must have a vision of growth rather than decay. One must put the temporary things, which grow older and die, in the right perspective. They are temporary. Spiritual things, though, are eternal. Aging and decay need not take us farther from God but can bring us closer. We move away from that which is temporary to that which is eternal. We grow stronger while growing weaker.

Living in the Present While Looking to the Future (5:1–8)

One man, frustrated with not having his needs met, said, "I don't want to hear about pie in the sky in the bye and bye. I want something sound on the ground while I'm still around." Paul not only was assured of something sound on the ground while he was still around, but also he was looking forward to something sound in the bye and bye.

In 5:1, Paul contrasted the present human body with the future heavenly body. He likened the earthly body to a "tent" and the heavenly body to a "building." While the earthly body is temporary and can be destroyed, the heavenly body is eternal, not built with human hands.

We often speak of living in the present as "life." Paul spoke of it as being "mortal" (5:4). He saw being "mortal" as leading to death. But he

Guaranteed

What does Paul mean in 2 Corinthians 5:5 about the *guarantee* of what is to come? What is guaranteed is our heavenly body and heavenly dwelling. How is this guarantee made? The English word "guaranteeing" is the translation of a form of the Greek word *arrabon*. The word signifies the down payment or earnest money that one gives assuring the recipient of final payment in full.

John wrote, "This is how we know that he lives in us: We know it by the Spirit he gave us" (1 John 3:24). The Holy Spirit initially connects the believer to Jesus Christ (Titus 3:5) and then becomes the assurance that the believer is connected eternally. The Holy Spirit brings the life of Jesus to the believer and gradually transforms the believer into the likeness of Jesus. This is God's purpose for God's people. God guarantees it by his Holy Spirit.

---

described eternity as "life." Eternity is life because it is in eternity that we are "clothed with our heavenly dwelling" (5:4). So, while Paul was living in the present, he was looking to the future.

Paul's idea of being clothed and "not be found naked" would be a mystery to the Greek mind in Corinth (5:3). The Greeks did not believe in a bodily life after death. They taught that death released the immortal soul from a dying body. The soul would then be absorbed into the divine. Paul wrote, though, that in death he would have a body, one that would be made by God and would be eternal, not temporary. He would not be going around heaven "naked" as a disembodied soul.

Troubles can either beat us down or fire us up.

In Philippians 1:21–23, Paul expressed this same idea of living in the present while looking to the future. He wrote in verse 21, "For to me, to live is Christ and to die is gain." Eternal life for Paul was not only a quantity of life but also a quality of life. The eternal life of Jesus had entered Paul on the road to Damascus. Paul was experiencing eternal life while living in a fleshly body, and he would experience fully eternal life living in a heavenly body. The presence of God that Paul experienced in life would not be broken by death.

Our six-year-old granddaughter Olivia had spent the week with us. We attended the Houston Rodeo and Fair, where she ate what she wanted, rode all the rides she wanted, and watched the rodeo. When it came time for us to take her back home to her parents in Austin, she was in a dilemma. She wanted to go and see her parents, but she wanted to stay with us. She worried all morning as we prepared to drive from Houston to Austin. She asked us over and over again to help her make up her mind whether to stay or go. All the way to Austin, a three-hour drive, she debated the issue. We flipped a coin and called heads or tails to help make a decision. Finally I told her to take a piece of paper and put a line down the middle. On one side of the line, she was to put all the reasons she wanted to go home and on the other side, to put all the reasons she wanted to stay. That exercise lasted for some time, but it ultimately resulted in a tie. When we got her home to Austin, she was thrilled to see her parents. But when her grandmother and I left, she cried.

> The believer grows stronger while growing weaker by having a different vision of life and death.

This seems to be our dilemma as Christians. We want to go and be with the Lord, but we also want to stay and be with our family and friends. This was Paul's dilemma.

Paul stated in verse 7 that believers "live by faith, not by sight." We know what we have in this life, and we know what we are promised in the life to come. We live in the present while looking to the future.

Pleasing God While Expecting What Is Due (5:9–10)

My mother was the most important person in my life. Her love, care, and guidance helped shape my life. She was a great spiritual leader and example. She not only taught me to be my best, but she helped me be my best. The person I most wanted to please in life was my mother.

"We Do Not Lose Heart"

A woman in our church was diagnosed with cancer and spent many months in a hospital receiving treatment. Every time I would visit Mamie, her husband Ike would say, "Mamie, Phil's here." She would always open her eyes and greet me. One day, I entered the room, and Ike said, "Mamie, Phil's here." Mamie didn't respond. Ike said, "Phil's here," several more times.

Finally, Mamie, who had been turned toward the wall, turned toward me and said, "Well, Phil, what do you think God thinks about this now?"

How would you have responded to her, based on Paul's statement to the Corinthians that "we do not lose heart" (2 Cor. 4:16)?

Paul emphasized in verse 9 that pleasing God took precedence over everything else for him. In fact, Paul wrote that he made it his "goal" to please God. He had already stated that he was guaranteed a heavenly body and a heavenly home, but he did not take that guarantee as an opportunity to do his own thing. He recognized that as a believer he would be held accountable for his actions.

Paul had written about personal accountability in 1 Corinthians (1 Corinthians 3:10–15). In that letter he used the concept of building a structure with different kinds of materials. A life built with deeds pleasing to God is represented by gold, silver, and costly stones. A life built with deeds not pleasing to God is represented by wood, hay, and straw. Paul taught that a day will come in every believer's life when his or her actions on earth will be judged. Only those actions that are pleasing to God will survive for eternity.

Paul not only was assured of something sound on the ground while he was still around, but also he was looking forward to something sound in the bye and bye.

Several years ago I was asked to lead the memorial service for one of my college football coaches. He and I had remained close friends beyond my college years. He often told me that if he died before I died, he wanted me to lead his memorial service. One of the things that I shared in that service was the great love the athletes felt for this particular coach. He was one of the toughest coaches I knew. Yet, no matter how rough he had been on each one of us during practice, he never let us leave the football field until he had put his arm around us to let us know how much we were loved. He gave us the confidence that, even though he would judge our actions, he always loved and accepted us.

Paul allowed his actions to be guided by two spiritual principles: the judgment of God and the love of God.

Practical Applications for Today

One of the most powerful testimonies to a living Jesus is a positive attitude in the face of age, decay, and trouble. As believers, we do not deny the reality of growing older and weaker. Neither do we deny problems or the pain they bring. We look beyond those problems to the living Lord Jesus and the strength the Lord gives to live with aging, decay, and trouble. We know that growing older simply brings us closer to our heavenly body and home.

God "has given the Spirit as a deposit, guaranteeing what is to come"—our heavenly body and heavenly home (2 Cor. 5:5). The Spirit also is a guide to our earthly behavior. He is the one who convinces us to live a life pleasing to God. Even though we are eternally accepted by God through our faith in Jesus Christ, we are accountable to God for how we live our earthly lives.

QUESTIONS

1. What causes you to "lose heart"?

2. In what ways does God renew you every day?

3. How do you fix your eyes on what is unseen?

4. What are some elements in a life pleasing to God?

Focal Text

2 Corinthians 5:11–21

Background

2 Corinthians 5:11–21

Main Idea

What God has done for us in Christ should be more than sufficient to motivate us to minister.

Question to Explore

What does it take to get you motivated?

Study Aim

To decide on ways I will respond to God's motivations to ministry

Study and Action Emphases

- Affirm the Bible as our authoritative guide for life and ministry
- Share the gospel with all people
- Develop a growing, vibrant faith
- Obey and serve Jesus by meeting physical, spiritual, and emotional needs
- Equip people for servant leadership

LESSON SIX

Motivated to Minister

Quick Read

Paul was trying to commend Christ, not himself, to the Corinthian believers. He urged them to get motivated to share this love of Christ, since they were a new creation and no longer lived for themselves but for Christ.

We sometimes say, *That person lacks motivation.* So what do we mean? We may mean we think the person is lazy—unless we are talking about ourselves! In a positive sense, what we likely mean is that the person lacks sufficient good cause to do whatever it is we think the person ought to do. This passage in 2 Corinthians reminds us that Christians have ample reasons to minister. Paul said it's time to get motivated.

2 Corinthians 5:11–21

[11]Since, then, we know what it is to fear the Lord, we try to persuade men. What we are is plain to God, and I hope it is also plain to your conscience. [12]We are not trying to commend ourselves to you again, but are giving you an opportunity to take pride in us, so that you can answer those who take pride in what is seen rather than in what is in the heart. [13]If we are out of our mind, it is for the sake of God; if we are in our right mind, it is for you. [14]For Christ's love compels us, because we are convinced that one died for all, and therefore all died. [15]And he died for all, that those who live should no longer live for themselves but for him who died for them and was raised again.

[16]So from now on we regard no one from a worldly point of view. Though we once regarded Christ in this way, we do so no longer. [17]Therefore, if anyone is in Christ, he is a new creation; the old has gone, the new has come! [18]All this is from God, who reconciled us to himself through Christ and gave us the ministry of reconciliation: [19]that God was reconciling the world to himself in Christ, not counting men's sins against them. And he has committed to us the message of reconciliation. [20]We are therefore Christ's ambassadors, as though God were making his appeal through us. We implore you on Christ's behalf: Be reconciled to God. [21]God made him who had no sin to be sin for us, so that in him we might become the righteousness of God.

Motivated by Accountability to God and Others (5:11–13)

After Paul came to know Jesus personally, he understood that he would be accountable to Jesus for eternity. This knowledge motivated Paul not only to live his life to please God, but to "persuade" others to accept Jesus and live for God.

Paul's understanding of his accountability was expressed in the words "to fear the Lord" (5:11). In this context the word "fear" does not mean so much *to be afraid* but *to respect.* This "fear" keeps people from doing things that would break the heart of one they love. This same Greek word is translated "respect" in 1 Peter 2:18, "Slaves, submit yourselves to your masters with all respect. . . ." Paul respected the authority of God. He knew that he was not only under the care of God but also he was under the authority of God. He had already written that "we must all appear before the judgment seat of Christ" to give an account of our deeds, both good and bad (2 Cor. 5:10). Paul's great respect for God motivated him to live a life pleasing to God. See Proverbs 9:10; 19:23.

I grew up with great respect for my mother and father. They loved me and cared for me. They taught me personal responsibility and accountability. When I was an elementary student, my mother gave me the responsibility of riding my bicycle five miles from our house to a neighborhood grocery store to pay our monthly grocery bill and bring back the cash from my father's paycheck. I was excited and scared as I set out on that journey. I could imagine someone trying to rob me as I returned home with all the cash our family possessed. I was very pleased that my mother and father trusted me that much, but I was also afraid of failing. After I returned home safely, I felt much pride in my ability to do what was expected. Too, my love and respect for my parents grew from that experience.

Paul felt that his responsibility to God extended beyond himself to others. In 2 Corinthians 5:11–13, Paul explained that he was not trying to "commend" himself, but that he was being transparent to God and the Corinthians, for the sake of persuading others to accept Jesus as Savior. Paul knew that not only he must face the judgment of God but also so would everyone else (5:10).

. . . It's time to get motivated.

Paul's persuasiveness may have caused some to consider him to be out of his mind (5:13; see Acts 26:24). However, Paul had already documented some personal spiritual experiences in the first Corinthian letter (1 Corinthians 14:18). He did so again in this second letter (2 Cor. 12:1–7). These intense personal experiences came as a result of Paul's personal relationship with God, and they were between him and God. But Paul stated that in his work with the Corinthians, he was very rational. He was in his right mind for them.

Living a life pleasing to God may cause some to think we are out of our minds. But knowing that Jesus is counting on us should motivate us to live this kind of life. Too, knowing that others will face an accounting for their lives should motivate us to share the gospel with them in a clear and rational way.

Motivated by the Love of Christ (5:14–17)

There's an old saying that "love makes the world go round." One pundit changed the saying to "Love may not make the world go round, but it makes the trip worthwhile." This passage in 2 Corinthians would certainly echo the second statement. The supreme motive for Paul's ministry was the love of Christ.

When Paul wrote about the motivating love of Christ, he used the word "compels" (5:14). The New English Bible translates the Greek word with the phrase "leaves us no choice." This Greek word can also be translated *control* or *rule*. Paul's ministry was *controlled* or *ruled* by the love of Christ. He was left with "no choice" but to share the love of Christ that he had experienced. In Acts 18:5, Luke wrote that "Paul devoted himself exclusively to preaching, testifying to the Jews that Jesus was the Christ." There, this same word used by Paul in 2 Corinthians 5:14 is translated as "devoted himself exclusively." It is clear from the different translations of this word that Paul's primary motivation for ministry was the love of Christ.

Paul's great respect for God motivated him to live a life pleasing to God.

In Romans 5:8, Paul wrote, "God demonstrates his own love for us in this: While we were still sinners, Christ died for us." The knowledge that Christ could love Paul, "the worst" of sinners (1 Timothy 1:15), absolutely overwhelmed him and compelled him to minister for the sake of Christ. Again, in Romans 8:39, Paul wrote that nothing would be able to separate a believer from "the love of God that is in Christ Jesus our Lord." The wonderful security of the love of Christ left Paul no choice but to minister.

Christ's love for each one of us should be a primary motive for ministry. When we consider that each of us is a sinner, that the wages of sin is death, but that the gift of God is eternal life through Jesus Christ, we should feel compelled to minister.

Paul was convinced that Christ's death was not exclusively for him but for "all" (2 Cor. 5:14). For this reason, he regarded "no one from a worldly point of view" (5:16). He had at one time "regarded Christ in this way" (5:16). Years earlier, the Pharisaical Paul had judged Jesus and his followers by human standards. Because of this, Paul had tried to eliminate Christianity by persecuting and killing those who followed Christ. But now Paul viewed everyone from his perspective of the new birth in Jesus

Christ. He wrote (5:17), "If anyone is in Christ, he is a new creation; the old has gone, the new has come!"

Paul was a "new creation." When Christ died on the cross, Paul died with him (5:14). When Christ rose from the dead, Paul rose with him. Since Paul rose with Christ, the life Paul lived now was lived for Christ. All these things were true for all who accepted Jesus Christ as Savior.

Paul knew that not only he must face the judgment of God but also so would everyone else (5:10).

The love that Christ had for all, a love that led Christ to die for the sins of all, motivated Paul to minister to all. He was convinced of the possibility of all coming to faith in Christ. He felt indebted to all to preach the good news of Jesus Christ (Rom. 1:14–15). He was "not ashamed of the gospel" because he knew it was "the power of God for the salvation of everyone who believes" (Rom. 1:16).

Do you know someone who needs to become a "new creation" (2 Cor. 5:17)? That should motivate you to share the love of Christ with them. It certainly motivated Paul.

Motivated by the Commission of God (5:18–21)

God has commissioned every believer to be an ambassador for the good news. Paul wrote that God has "committed to us the message of reconciliation" (5:19). What is the message of reconciliation, and what does it mean that this message has been committed to us?

God Made Jesus "to Be Sin"?

What does it mean that God made Jesus "to be sin" (2 Cor. 5:21)? Paul wrote that God made him "to be sin," not to *be a sinner*. This distinction is very crucial. God does not make anyone sin.

Jesus never knew sin the way we do, by sinning. Jesus was tempted to sin but never sinned (Hebrews 4:15). Jesus continued to be sinless through the experience of the cross. In the experience of the cross, though, Jesus became the sin offering for us. God placed on Jesus the sin of us all (Isaiah 53:6), so that Jesus took our sins in his own body on the cross (1 Peter 2:24). In doing this, Jesus became "a curse for us" (Galatians 3:13). Jesus was charged with our guilt and penalty. God made Jesus "to be sin" for us so that we might become God's righteousness in relationship with Jesus.

The message of reconciliation is that God "reconciled us to himself through Christ" (5:18). The Greek word translated "reconciled" means *being put into friendship with God.* Why would a person need to be put into friendship with God? According to Romans 5:10, before Christ died for our sins "we were God's enemies." God was not our enemy, but we were God's enemy. Our evil behavior indicated that in our minds we were enemies of God (Colossians 1:21).

God did not erect the barriers between himself and human beings. People did. God took the initiative to make us his friends. God did this through the physical death of Jesus (Col. 1:22). God's reconciliation consisted of "not counting men's sins against them" (2 Cor. 5:19). God canceled the debt in his ledger by blotting it out with Christ's blood (Col. 2:14). Christ's death on the cross gave believers credit for their sin debt. Paul wrote, "God made him who had no sin to be sin for us, so that in him we might become the righteousness of God" (2 Cor. 5:21). When a person accepts Jesus Christ as Savior, that person's sins are counted as paid by the death of Jesus. The believer is then given the righteous life of Christ. Instead of counting our sins against us, God counts our faith for us.

> *The love that Christ had for all, a love that led Christ to die for the sins of all, motivated Paul to minister to all.*

God has committed to believers this message of reconciliation. It was not to angels or spirits, but to "us," human beings, that God committed this eternal message (5:19). When people have experienced the reconciliation of God through Jesus Christ, then they are obligated to share their experience with others. Paul wrote that we are "therefore Christ's ambassadors" (5:20). Ambassadors are people who represent their government and speak for their ruler. Ambassadors don't offer their own thoughts but those of their superior. Ambassadors are absolutely responsible to their superior. The message Christ's ambassadors carry is one of amnesty to

An Action Plan

- Write a brief testimony of how you came to faith in Christ.
- Name some of the characteristics of a "new creation" in Christ (2 Cor. 5:17).
- Design a strategy for your sharing the message of reconciliation.
- Make a list of those you know need to be reconciled to God.
- Set a goal for sharing the message of reconciliation.

those who are guilty of sin against God. This is the message God has committed to believers.

While studying at seminary I had the privilege of serving as an associate pastor to a wonderful pastor of a large church. The church provided transportation to Sunday services for those who needed it.

One Sunday morning an adult man responded to the invitation of the pastor to accept Christ as Savior. I was given the opportunity of talking with the man about his commitment to Christ. He had not come to this church before. His young daughter and her mother had been riding the bus to church on Sunday morning.

> *His young daughter had been an ambassador for Christ, and her father had become a believer.*

When I asked him how he came to know Jesus Christ personally, he unfolded a piece of construction paper. On the paper was a picture of Jesus with little children. This man's young daughter had colored the picture with crayon. Printed at the bottom of the paper was John 3:16. The man pointed at the Scripture and began to cry. His young daughter had been an ambassador for Christ, and her father had become a believer.

Summary

Paul became a new creation on the road to Damascus. He was changed from being an enemy of God to being a friend of God. The love of God in Christ was so overwhelming that it compelled Paul to share the news with everyone. He was convinced that Christ died for everyone. He no longer looked at Christ or people from a "worldly point of view" (2 Cor. 5:16). He saw the possibility of reconciliation for everyone. He considered himself and other believers as ambassadors for Christ. He actually felt that God was making his appeal through reconciled people.

Implications for Today

God's plan for sharing the good news of reconciliation centers in reconciled people. The forgiving work God did through the death and resurrection of Jesus Christ should motivate those who believe to share the good news. The fact that Jesus died for all means that all are potential recipients of God's reconciliation. The love of Christ for each one of us and the need for reconciliation for all of us should motivate us to minister.

QUESTIONS

1. In what ways do our lifestyles convince people that we are believers?

2. What is the difference between promoting ourselves and promoting Jesus Christ?

3. How do we demonstrate that the love of Christ is the premier love of our life?

4. What are some ways that we judge others by worldly standards?

5. What is an example of being an ambassador for Christ?

Focal Text

2 Corinthians
6:1–13; 7:2–4

Background

2 Corinthians 6:1—7:4

Main Idea

Personal example and
honest relationships are
powerful instruments
of ministry.

Question to Explore

What does your example
and your conversation
say to others?

Study Aim

To summarize Paul's description of his ministry
and his plea to the Corinthians and state
implications for my life today

Study and Action Emphases

- Affirm the Bible as our authoritative guide for
  life and ministry
- Share the gospel with all people
- Develop a growing, vibrant faith
- Include all God's family in decision-making
  and service
- Value all people as created in the image of God
- Equip people for servant leadership

LESSON SEVEN

Be Faithful, Be Real

Quick Read

There is an old saying, "He is more mask than
face," meaning that a person is not authentic.
Paul made himself transparent to establish an
authentic faith relationship with the Corinthian
church.

I was once a guest at a luncheon honoring two major university football teams. The head coach of one of the teams was introducing his punter, a Kodak® College All-American. The coach told the young man to stand. Then he shared a story of this young man's mother and her sacrifice to help her son go to a major college. The coach related how this young man's single mom had worked two jobs so her son could begin his college career.

The young man began to cry as the coach spoke. Suddenly the coach paused and said, "Son, I'm not saying this to embarrass you, but to show these people what a great mother you have." Paul was not making himself transparent to embarrass the Corinthian believers but to show them what a great message he had brought them. It was the message of salvation through faith in Jesus Christ.

2 Corinthians 6:1–13

[1]As God's fellow workers we urge you not to receive God's grace in vain. [2]For he says,
"In the time of my favor I heard you,
and in the day of salvation I helped you."
I tell you, now is the time of God's favor, now is the day of salvation. [3]We put no stumbling block in anyone's path, so that our ministry will not be discredited. [4]Rather, as servants of God we commend ourselves in every way: in great endurance; in troubles, hardships and distresses; [5]in beatings, imprisonments and riots; in hard work, sleepless nights and hunger; [6]in purity, understanding, patience and kindness; in the Holy Spirit and in sincere love; [7]in truthful speech and in the power of God; with weapons of righteousness in the right hand and in the left; [8]through glory and dishonor, bad report and good report; genuine, yet regarded as impostors; [9]known, yet regarded as unknown; dying, and yet we live on; beaten, and yet not killed; [10]sorrowful, yet always rejoicing; poor, yet making many rich; having nothing, and yet possessing everything.

[11]We have spoken freely to you, Corinthians, and opened wide our hearts to you. [12]We are not withholding our affection from you, but you are withholding yours from us. [13]As a fair exchange—I speak as to my children—open wide your hearts also.

2 Corinthians 7:2–4

[2]Make room for us in your hearts. We have wronged no one, we have corrupted no one, we have exploited no one. [3]I do not say this to

> condemn you; I have said before that you have such a place in our hearts that we would live or die with you. ⁴I have great confidence in you; I take great pride in you. I am greatly encouraged; in all our troubles my joy knows no bounds.

Transparency Before Trust (6:1–2)

In 2 Corinthians 5:11, Paul asserted that he was open before God and that he hoped he was open before the Corinthians. He understood how important it was to be transparent as he tried to establish the gospel in the Corinthian church. There was an urgency about this gospel message. Paul was communicating the message of God's grace (2 Corinthians 6:1–2). This grace had come through the life, death, and resurrection of Jesus. Paul referred to the "day of salvation" and said that that day is "now."

It would not last forever. Therefore, Paul urged the Corinthians not to take this day of grace lightly, living only for themselves or exchanging this gospel for another gospel (2 Cor. 11:4).

Paul chose to be honest about his troubles and accomplishments even at the risk of sounding as if he was bragging.

To "receive God's grace in vain" (6:1) did not mean that the Corinthians would lose their salvation, which came from receiving the gospel. Jesus made it clear that those who accepted him as Savior would be safe in his hands forever (John 10:28). To "receive God's grace in vain" meant that their profession of faith and their practice of that faith would be inconsistent.

Transparency and trust go hand in hand. It was Paul's purpose to "put no stumbling block in anyone's path" (2 Cor. 6:3). He did not want any hidden agenda to discredit his ministry. The Greek word for "discredit" implies mocking and ridicule. Paul did not want to give occasion for anyone to laugh at or make fun of his ministry.

Telling the truth does not necessarily mean telling everything. Every person has a right to some emotional privacy. Yet, hiding something pertinent to one's ministry is certain to discredit that ministry if ultimately revealed.

For instance, any Christian who constantly talks about his or her generosity toward those in need, while not actually giving to help those in need, will be discredited if found out. That was what happened to Judas. In John 12:4–6, Judas protested the waste of expensive perfume on the anointing of Jesus. He claimed that the perfume could have been sold and the money given to the poor. But John wrote, "He did not say this because he cared about the poor, but because he was a thief; as keeper of the money bag, he used to help himself to what was put into it" (John 12:6). Judas was hiding something pertinent to his ministry. Ultimately, his duplicity, which led him to betray Jesus for money, also led to his suicide.

Transparency, or openness, is crucial to trust. People may not agree with everything you stand for, but if you are transparent, they will trust you.

Transparency as Commendation (6:3–10)

The old saying, "Honesty is the best policy," is true. Paul chose to be honest about his troubles and accomplishments even at the risk of sounding as if he was bragging. In our polite society, especially among Christians, it is considered rude to brag on oneself. Years ago an old football coach said of one of his players, "It ain't bragging if you can do it." Paul could do it and had done it. He shared what he had done as a commendation of his ministry to the Corinthians. He wanted their support, and he gave many reasons he should have their support.

Transparency and trust go hand in hand.

In 6:3–10, Paul commended his determination in sharing the gospel by pointing out both the suffering he had endured and the spiritual qualities

Freedom of Conscience

Thomas Helwys helped form the first Baptist church on English soil about 1611–12. Here he published a small book entitled *A Short Declaration of the Mystery of Iniquity*. It contained what would become a bedrock principle of Baptists, a call for freedom of conscience. He addressed his dedication to King James I, the King of England. In his address to the king, he stated that the king was a man and not God. He wrote that even though every citizen should be obedient to the king, the believer was ultimately responsible to God in spiritual matters.

This kind of transparency and "frank speech" landed Helwys in prison at Newgate, where he probably died. His openness and conviction, though, led Baptists to become noted as champions of freedom of conscience in spiritual matters.

that had sustained him in the suffering. In 6:4–5, Paul listed nine forms of suffering arranged in three sets of three, as follows:
- sufferings in general—"troubles, hardships and distresses"
- sufferings caused by others—"beatings, imprisonments and riots"
- sufferings from the work—"hard work, sleepless nights and hunger"

In 6:6–7, Paul pointed out the spiritual qualities that sustained him in the suffering: "purity, understanding, patience and kindness . . . the Holy Spirit . . . sincere love . . . truthful speech . . . the power of God" and "weapons of righteousness."

In 6:8–10, Paul summarized all this in pairs of antitheses. "Dishonor" and "bad report" are countered with "glory" and "good report." By the world, Paul was regarded as "unknown," "dying," "sorrowful," "poor," and "having nothing." But by the standards of the gospel, he was "known," lived on, rejoiced, and possessed everything. (See comments in lesson three about Paul's use of "we.")

Paul set a good example for us by commending himself to the Corinthians through being transparent about his strengths and weaknesses.

Sometimes believers may be hesitant about sharing strengths for fear someone will think they are bragging. Too, sometimes believers are hesitant about sharing their weaknesses for fear someone will think they are spiritually imma-ture. Trying to protect themselves from criticism may lead believers to be less than transparent. Trying to protect God from criticism can lead to the same result. Paul set a good example for us by commending himself to the Corinthians through being transparent about his strengths and weaknesses.

Transparency as Openness (6:11–13; 7:2–4)

Paul was quite open and frank about his affection for the Corinthians and their lack of affection for him (6:11–13; 7:2–4). Paul used a communication method known as "frank speech," which was accepted in his day but is not so familiar in our day. It is related to what Paul referred to in Ephesians 4:15, as "speaking the truth in love."

Frank speech was not speech designed to hurt but to help. Frank speech was openness in communication. (See "Introducing 2 Corinthians" for further comments on frank speech.)

Paul wanted the Corinthians to know how much he loved them and that he wanted them to return that love. He made it very plain that he had not taken advantage of his position by mistreating the Corinthians. Neither had he been open and honest—frank—in order to condemn them. Some might have taken his frank speech as an attempt to put them in their place. In fact, Paul made it clear that the Corinthian believers were so dear to him that he would "live or die" with them (7:3). Their place was in his heart.

Paul concluded this part of his "frank speech" with a strong and positive word of commendation. He reaffirmed his confidence and pride in the Corinthian believers, letting them know that he was "greatly encouraged" (7:4).

Paul was also very open and frank about the interpersonal relationships of believers with unbelievers (6:14—7:1). Note that Paul began this frank assessment with the term "yoked together" (6:14), stating that Christians should not be "yoked together with unbelievers."

What did Paul mean? Examining this passage along with other New Testament passages, we see that there needs to be a balance in how Christians relate to non-Christians. For instance, in 1 Corinthians 5:10–11, Paul admitted that one would have to leave the world not to associate with those who were unbelievers. When Jesus used the analogy of believers as "salt of the earth" (Matthew 6:13), it is obvious that salt must touch whatever it is to preserve. In 1 Corinthians 7:12–16, Paul admitted that a believer might win an unbelieving mate by staying in the marriage. He condoned a believer eating a meal with an unbeliever (1 Cor. 10:27).

Transparency as openness is crucial in all relationships, whether with believers or unbelievers.

These passages suggest that Paul accepted the person while not accepting the behavior. He was not approving of sin. He knew, though, that every person had worth, being created in the image of God. Therefore, it was not Christian to treat a non-Christian as a non-human. Paul knew that decency in personal relationships could create a bridge to reach a non-Christian with the gospel. That is why he wrote, "I have become all things to all men so that by all possible means I might save some" (1 Cor. 9:22).

The term "yoked together" defines how the relationships between believers and non-believers are to be handled. Paul made it plain that the believer must not be in a relationship that drags him or her along in the direction of the unbeliever. The picture is of two people in one yoke

Case Study

Frank was in his first pastorate out of the seminary. The church was beginning their annual budget promotion. Frank asked one of the noted members to be a spokesman. Upon hearing who the spokesman would be, the financial secretary came to Frank to tell him that this noted member did not support the church financially, even though most of the members assumed he did. How would you advise Pastor Frank to deal with this situation?

pulling together. A yoke was a kind of wooden harness that was used to join two oxen together so that they could work together in pulling a load. Using that image, Paul was saying that the believer should not be pulling the cargo of the unbeliever's unbelief. Why after taking the yoke of Jesus (Matthew 11:29) would the believer then want to throw it off and take the yoke of the unbeliever?

To contrast the two yokes, Paul asked five rhetorical questions, introduced by the Greek interrogative pronoun translated "what," preceding five successive synonyms translated "in common," "fellowship," "harmony," "in common," "agreement," followed by five antitheses—"righteousness and wickedness," light and darkness, "Christ and Belial," believer and unbeliever, "temple of God and idols" (6:14–16). Each of these questions asked by Paul presupposed a negative answer. Thus, the meaning is that these things are mutually exclusive. Since being "yoked together" could determine the future for the believer, Paul wanted to make the results very clear.

Honesty really is the best policy.

The story is told about a country preacher in the early days of automobiles when roads were mainly dirt. The roads turned to mud when it rained, and cars traveling the roads left deep ruts. As the preacher came to a fork in the dirt road, a sign read, "Be careful which ruts you get into, because you will be in them for the next twenty-five miles." This expresses some of the sentiment of Paul's admonition to the Corinthians to "not be yoked together with unbelievers."

Implications

Transparency as openness is crucial in all relationships, whether with believers or unbelievers. Transparency is not easy, however. Being open with others may not always be pleasant. However, openness and frankness don't have to mean rudeness. Telling the truth does not mean we have to expose totally everything about ourselves or about our lives to everyone in every circumstance.

Transparency does mean, however, that we are to be honest about ourselves, especially as related to our walk with the Lord. Being transparent builds trust among those we are seeking to influence. Being transparent also helps us to build bridges to those who are not believers. Honesty really is the best policy.

QUESTIONS

1. What are some common hypocrisies among believers?

2. What traits cause you to trust another believer?

3. What are some examples of Christian "frank speech"?

4. What are some areas where being "unequally yoked" is a temptation?

5. How can we build bridges to unbelievers without becoming "unequally yoked"?

Focal Text

2 Corinthians 7:5–16

Background

2 Corinthians 7:5–16

Main Idea

Learning to give and receive criticism in a positive manner is an integral part of Christian growth.

Question to Explore

How did you feel the last time someone criticized you? the last time you criticized someone else?

Study Aim

To summarize Paul's confrontation of the Corinthians and their reception of his criticism and identify implications for how I relate to other people

Study and Action Emphases

- Affirm the Bible as our authoritative guide for life and ministry
- Develop a growing, vibrant faith
- Include all God's family in decision-making and service
- Value all people as created in the image of God
- Encourage healthy families
- Obey and serve Jesus by meeting physical, spiritual, and emotional needs
- Equip people for servant leadership

LESSON EIGHT

Giving and Receiving Criticism

Quick Read

There are two types of criticism: constructive and destructive. We learn from Paul's relationship to the Corinthians how to give and how to receive constructive criticism.

One of the most influential teachers in my life was a middle-school speech teacher. She recognized that I had a gift for speaking, and she encouraged me to let her work with me to develop that gift. She was a very precise and demanding teacher. She took nothing for granted, including posture, eye contact, gestures, and voice modulation. Sometimes her criticisms hurt my feelings, but she always explained that she wanted to enhance a gift I already possessed. Even now, after serving as pastor for thirty-five years and speaking all over the world, I can hear her voice saying to me, "Don't cross your legs while sitting on the platform." This teacher entered me in an Optimist Oratorical Contest for middle-school students, where I won a trophy. Her constructive criticism has continued to pay rich dividends in my life for more than thirty-five years.

Paul's constructive criticism was painful for the Corinthians to hear. But their positive response to the criticism brought about productive changes in their lives.

The background of this section is found in 2 Corinthians 2:13, where Paul wrote that he could not rest in Troas because he didn't know how the situation in Corinth had developed. He had set out for Macedonia to meet Titus and find out as quickly as he could what was happening. Something had gone wrong in Corinth, and Paul had made a quick visit, which evidently only made matters worse. After his visit, he sent Titus to them with a strong letter that evidently brought a great deal of sorrow. In this part of the letter, Paul recounted his joy from Titus's report about the response of the Corinthians to the letter.

2 Corinthians 7:5–16

⁵For when we came into Macedonia, this body of ours had no rest, but we were harassed at every turn—conflicts on the outside, fears within. ⁶But God, who comforts the downcast, comforted us by the coming of Titus, ⁷and not only by his coming but also by the comfort you had given him. He told us about your longing for me, your deep sorrow, your ardent concern for me, so that my joy was greater than ever. ⁸Even if I caused you sorrow by my letter, I do not regret it. Though I did regret it—I see that my letter hurt you, but only for a little while—⁹yet now I am happy, not because you were made sorry, but because your sorrow led you to repentance. For you became sorrowful as God intended and so were not harmed in any way by us. ¹⁰Godly sorrow brings repentance that leads to salvation and leaves no regret, but worldly

sorrow brings death. [11]See what this godly sorrow has produced in you: what earnestness, what eagerness to clear yourselves, what indignation, what alarm, what longing, what concern, what readiness to see justice done. At every point you have proved yourselves to be innocent in this matter. [12]So even though I wrote to you, it was not on account of the one who did the wrong or of the injured party, but rather that before God you could see for yourselves how devoted to us you are. [13]By all this we are encouraged.

In addition to our own encouragement, we were especially delighted to see how happy Titus was, because his spirit has been refreshed by all of you. [14]I had boasted to him about you, and you have not embarrassed me. But just as everything we said to you was true, so our boasting about you to Titus has proved to be true as well. [15]And his affection for you is all the greater when he remembers that you were all obedient, receiving him with fear and trembling. [16]I am glad I can have complete confidence in you.

Criticism Can Be Painful (7:5–8)

This portion of 2 Corinthians gives us great insight into Paul's personality, his manner of leadership, and his deep concern for people. He was not deterred by personal pain or discomfort in his determination to spread the gospel (2 Corinthians 7:5). He had already enumerated for the Corinthian church the kinds of pain and discomfort he had experienced as a result of his ministry (2 Cor. 6:3–10). But along with the pain and discomfort, Paul took encouragement from his belief that God worked through his children to bring comfort in times of need (7:6).

The Corinthians had to accept responsibility for the problem before they could solve it.

Paul had such a forceful personality that he did not regret sending a painful letter to the Corinthians (7:8). Paul had such a deep concern for people that he was willing to be forceful and critical to bring attention to their sinful and destructive behavior. He recognized that there was a time when criticism was necessary.

We get another picture of this forceful personality in Paul's encounter with Peter recorded in Galatians 2:11–21. Paul wrote of his confrontation with Peter, "I opposed him to his face, because he was clearly in the wrong" (Galatians 2:11). Peter had ministered with Jesus, had been present on the mountain when Jesus was transfigured, had been commissioned to preach by Jesus, and had brought the first sermon in Jerusalem on Pentecost following the resurrection. It would have been easy for Paul to ignore Peter's hypocrisy given Peter's significant place in the formation of the early church. But Paul's deep concern for the Gentiles and his conviction of the truth motivated him to criticize Peter publicly for his behavior.

Not everyone has the personality to offer painful criticism. Some are pained at the thought of being critical of others, even if the criticism is needed. On the other hand, there are those, who like Paul, can "lower the boom" while not being adversely affected by criticism of themselves.

> ... *If we can view criticism as an attempt to help, we will be more able to respond productively.*

We are not told what was contained in this letter that brought sorrow to the Corinthians (7:8). Scholars give several possibilities. Some suggest that the reference is to 1 Corinthians, especially 5:1–4 dealing with sexual sin in the church. Others suggest the reference is to 2 Corinthians 10—13, dealing with false teachers. Still others suggest it was the letter mentioned in 2 Corinthians 2:3–8, dealing with the forgiveness of an errant church member. Whatever the case, the letter was painful to the recipients.

The intention of this letter was not to bring pain, but to bring accountability (7:8–9). The Corinthians had to accept responsibility for the problem before they could solve it. Trying to avoid the pain that comes from confronting a problem by blaming others for the problem will never help us solve the problem.

A medical doctor may cause us pain trying to diagnose a problem. He or she may press or push on a sensitive area of our body to locate the source and intensity of the problem. The attempt to diagnose may be painful but very necessary.

Several years ago I suffered a bite from a brown recluse spider. I didn't know what had bitten me, but as the skin began to turn black around the bite, I knew I needed to see a doctor. The doctor diagnosed the bite and then took a small knife to probe the wound. He said to me, "I have to go down far enough to find healthy skin in order to treat this bite. It may be a little painful." He was right on both points. His critical work was painful. The pain resulted in healing, though.

Paul's criticism was painful, but it became productive in the lives of the Corinthians.

Criticism Can Be Productive (7:9–11)

Paul's letter produced a grief that led the Corinthians to make some necessary and positive changes (7:9–11). Paul was aware that sorrow brought on by criticism could lead in one of two directions, depending on the response of the one who was made sorry. It could turn one around, or it could grind one down. There was a sorrow that led to death, called "worldly sorrow" (7:10), and there was a sorrow that led to repentance and salvation, called "godly sorrow" (7:10). Worldly sorrow was a sorrow that made a person sad but brought about no change.

Two biblical examples of this sorrow are seen in the lives of Cain and Judas. When God rejected Cain's offering, while accepting his brother Abel's offering, Cain became angry and his face was "downcast" (Genesis 4:5). The "downcast" face represented sadness. God then told Cain that if he would change and do right he would be accepted. Cain was sad, but he rejected God's criticism and immediately killed his brother Abel. This murder caused Cain to become "a restless wanderer on the earth" (Genesis 4:14). He was sorry that his offering was not accepted, but he was not sorry enough to make the changes God told him to make. This is the "worldly sorrow" Paul noted in this passage.

Trying to avoid the pain that comes from confronting a problem by blaming others for the problem will never help us solve the problem.

The other example of "worldly sorrow" comes from the life of the disciple Judas. Judas sold Jesus to the Jewish religious leaders for thirty pieces of silver (Matthew 27:3). When Judas saw that Jesus was going to be killed, he was "seized with remorse" (Matt. 27:3). He tried to return the money to the religious authorities. The religious authorities told Judas that his sorrow was not their problem. Judas then went out and hanged himself (Matthew 27:5). Judas was sorry for what he did, but his sorrow, a worldly sorrow, led to his death.

There was not only a sorrow that led to death, but there was also a sorrow that led to repentance and salvation (2 Cor. 7:10). Paul called this sorrow "godly sorrow." Godly sorrow was a gift of God. It was the gift of God's permission to change one's mind and behavior. The New Testament word for this change is *repentance*. The Greek word for repentance is a compound word made up of two Greek words, meaning *to change the mind*. It came to mean not only to change the mind but also to change the behavior and the direction of one's life.

Godly sorrow is demonstrated in the lives of two prominent biblical characters, David and Peter. David, the king of Israel, committed adultery with Bathsheba, the wife of Uriah. Uriah was a leader of David's army (2 Samuel 11). Bathsheba became pregnant as a result of this relationship. In order to cover up his sin, David had Uriah put into the front of the battle, where he was killed. David thought this had solved his problem. But God revealed David's sin to the prophet Nathan. When Nathan the prophet confronted David with his sin, David became sorrowful. David repented and changed his behavior (2 Sam. 12; Psalm 51). Nathan did not confront David with criticism in order to destroy him but to redeem him. His words were truth offered in love. His criticism brought about a positive change in David's life.

Another example of "godly sorrow" is in the life of the disciple Simon Peter. The night Jesus was taken into custody by an armed group, a young girl confronted Peter and accused him of being a companion of Jesus. Peter denied that he knew Jesus (Matt. 26:70). Following this denial, the rooster crowed, fulfilling Jesus' prophecy that Peter would deny him three times before the rooster crowed (Matt. 26:75). Peter went out and wept bitterly, sorry that he had betrayed Jesus. Later, after the resurrection, Jesus came to the disciples on the Sea of Galilee. He confronted Peter in a positive way by asking Peter three times whether Peter loved him. Peter was "hurt" by Jesus' confrontation with him (John 21:17). Peter's pain, though, led him to repent and recommit his life to Jesus. Jesus did not confront Peter in order to condemn him but to restore him. Jesus' words were truth offered in love.

Criticism can even be destructive when it is offered with the best of intentions.

There is a sorrow that leads to death, and there is a sorrow that leads to repentance and salvation. The sorrow that leads to repentance and salvation leaves no regret (2 Cor. 7:10).

If we view criticism as a personal attack, we will rush to defend ourselves. However, if we can view criticism as an attempt to help, we will be more able to respond productively.

Criticism Can Be Providential (7:11–16)

Paul reminded the Corinthians that they "became sorrowful as God intended and so were not harmed in any way by us" (7:9). God provides constructive criticism intentionally in several ways. In the Corinthian letter we see how God provided providential criticism through the Apostle Paul. Providential criticism is offered to correct destructive behavior and provide positive guidance.

In Paul's second letter to Timothy, he reminded Timothy that God provided providential criticism through Scripture (2 Timothy 3:16–17). Paul wrote that Scripture is useful for "rebuking, correcting and training in righteousness" (2 Tim. 3:16). He then added that the purpose of the criticism is that the "man of God may be thoroughly equipped for every good work." God's providential criticism is given to help Christians be more productive in God's work.

The writer of Hebrews described the Scriptures as "sharper than any double-edged sword," judging "the thoughts and intents of the heart" (Hebrews 4:12–13). Jesus taught the disciples that the Holy Spirit would "convict the world of guilt in regard to sin and righteous and judgment" (John 16:7–8). This providential criticism is designed to produce the positive changes Paul listed in 2 Corinthians 7:11: "earnestness," "eagerness to clear yourselves," "indignation," "alarm," "concern," and "readiness to see justice done."

The Corinthians were so appreciative of Paul's providential and corrective word that they actually lifted Titus's spirit when he visited them as Paul's representative (2 Cor. 7:13). Instead of attacking Titus, they received him with respect (7:15). They comforted and encouraged him (7:7). Paul became so excited about the response of the Corinthians to

"Worldly Sorrow"

Paul used the phrase "worldly sorrow" to describe the pain that resulted in regret but not in change (2 Cor. 7:10). The word "worldly" is used to describe the response of one who does not respond spiritually to criticism. "Worldly sorrow" is grief or pain at being caught or having one's attention brought to a need for corrective action. It is the pain of regret that one has been found out. "Worldly sorrow" is not sad over the activity that needs to be corrected but over the consequences of that activity. It is characterized by resentment at being criticized and bitterness over being punished. Paul used the word "regret" to describe this resentment (7:10).

In the movie version of *War and Peace*, the character Pierre shrugged off a night of wild living by saying, "I have sinned, Lord, but I have several excellent excuses." "Worldly sorrow" has several excellent excuses but no desire or intention to change. It eventually leads to death.

Titus that he boasted of his "complete confidence" in them (7:16). This confidence was probably short-lived if 2 Corinthians 10—13 reflects the situation after 2 Corinthians 1—9.

Another example of providential criticism is found in the lives of Cornelius and Simon Peter (Acts 10). While Peter was praying, God gave him a vision of all kinds of animals and commanded him to get up and eat. Peter, being a devout Jew, told the Lord that he would never eat anything "impure or unclean" (Acts 10:14). A voice spoke to him and told him not to call anything God had cleansed impure. Later Peter showed up at the home of Cornelius, who was a God-fearing man and a centurion in the Italian regiment. The Holy Spirit spoke to Peter and told him to accept Cornelius because the Spirit had sent him. It was through this experience that Peter would say, "I now realize how true it is that God does not show favoritism but accepts men from every nation who fear him and do what is right" (Acts 10:34–35).

> *One size does not fit all when it comes to receiving criticism.*

God's providential criticism helped Peter move beyond his religious discrimination, which kept him from associating with non-Jews. God's providential criticism also helped Peter become a more effective leader of the early church.

Implications for Today

There come times in life when criticism is necessary. The parent who does not exercise discipline and control in the life of a child for fear of the pain it may cause is forfeiting parental responsibility and inviting greater trouble down the road. A church that does not deal with a perilous situation in a timely fashion can find itself destroyed by that situation.

Criticism, however, must be handled very wisely. It has the potential to improve life or to destroy life.

Criticism generally is painful. The pain, though, can draw attention to areas of life that need to be changed and thus be constructive.

On the other hand, criticism can be destructive even when it is called "constructive criticism" by the one who is giving it. Criticism can be destructive in the way it is offered and be aimed at tearing someone down rather than improving the situation. Criticism can even be destructive when it is offered with the best of intentions. Everyone does not receive criticism in the same way. The slightest hint of a negative word may make a person of one personality type feel completely rejected while another person will pay little attention to a much more critical message. One size does not fit all when it comes to receiving criticism.

As we reflect on Paul's letter to the Corinthians, we can examine our willingness to give or receive criticism. His letter helps us see that criticism given in the right way and received in the right spirit has the power to change lives for the better. Before we offer personal criticism, we should think about our motives, though. Jesus reminded his disciples that they should first "take the plank" out of their own eye so that they "could see clearly to remove the speck" from their brother's eye (Matthew 7:5).

Should we look at constructive criticism as a word from the Lord for our benefit?

My wife and I had just bought our first house in a lovely neighborhood in Fort Worth, Texas. We had lived there only a few days and had not had opportunity to meet our neighbors. While driving home one day, we approached a man mowing his yard several houses from our new house. He was riding a lawnmower while mowing a very small yard. I launched into a critical word about how lazy some people were to ride a lawnmower to mow such a small yard. As we passed the man on the mower, my wife and I both noticed that he had no legs. After a brief moment of silence, my wife looked at me and said, "And you were saying?"

When offering a word of criticism, are we really trying to help someone or are we trying to put someone in his or her place or to get something "off our chest"? Is our criticism providential, guided by God's word and God's Spirit? Are we "speaking the truth in love" (Ephesians 4:15)?

When receiving criticism, does the criticism cause us to become sad to our own detriment?[1] Should we look at constructive criticism as a word from the Lord for our benefit?

QUESTIONS

1. What benefits can come from criticism within a family?

2. Who has the right to offer criticism in a family?

3. In what ways can a church benefit from constructive criticism?

4. How should a person respond to criticism?

5. What are some good ways to offer criticism?

6. What are some ways to avoid being destructive in giving criticism?

7. Why are people afraid to give criticism?

NOTES

1. For additional help on responding to criticism, especially in the workplace, see chapter 5, "Handle Criticism Carefully," in *How to Be Happier in the Job You Sometimes Can't Stand* by Ross West (Nashville, Tennessee: Broadman and Holman Publishers, 1998).

Learning to Give

Unless you learn how to be a giving person, you cannot be an obedient follower of Jesus Christ. You gain value as you learn to be a giving person. You are more valuable to everyone if you are a giving person.

You do not have to erase your financial portfolio to be a follower of Jesus Christ. You do, however, have to consider whether you are willing to be moved by the compassion of Christ to the point that your finances become a resource for God's kingdom.

When you begin taking ministry personally, by being the presence of Christ to others, you begin to live sacrificially. Christ does not call you to live in a self-punishing manner. Christ, though, does call you to ask yourself questions about your motives, your priorities, your values, and your will. To follow Christ is to ask yourself continually: *Am I willing to will God's will in my life?*

As you follow Jesus Christ, you take on Christ's character and spirit. You become moved with compassion more and more. Increasingly, maturing disciples of Jesus Christ are willing to live sacrificially in order to minister to the needs of other people.

In 2 Corinthians 8—9, Paul challenged followers of Christ to contribute to the needs of others. Specifically, Paul challenged the church in Corinth to help with the needs of the poor believers in Jerusalem. Paul expected the Corinthian Christians to be moved with compassion. Now Paul's words about giving come to you as Scripture, the written word of God.[1]

UNIT TWO, LEARNING TO GIVE

NOTES

1. Unless otherwise indicated, all Scripture quotations in unit two are from The Holy Bible, New International Version (North American Edition), copyright © 1973, 1978, 1984 by the International Bible Society. Used by permission of Zondervan Publishing House.

Focal Text

2 Corinthians 8:1–21

Background

2 Corinthians 8

Main Idea

Compelling reasons call us to decide to give of our financial resources to the Lord's work.

Question to Explore

How well does your financial giving match New Testament teachings?

Study Aim

To identify reasons for giving financially and evaluate their importance in my life

Study and Action Emphases

- Affirm the Bible as our authoritative guide for life and ministry
- Share the gospel with all people
- Develop a growing, vibrant faith
- Include all God's family in decision-making and service
- Value all people as created in the image of God
- Obey and serve Jesus by meeting physical, spiritual, and emotional needs
- Equip people for servant leadership

LESSON NINE

Reasons for Giving

Quick Read

If you expect to become more like Jesus Christ, taking ministry personally, you will need to learn New Testament reasons for being a giving person.

After their boat capsized, two men found themselves stranded on a deserted island. One fellow was depressed while the other was upbeat. After a few minutes, the depressed man asked the other, "How can you be so positive? Don't you know we will never be found? We are going to perish on this forsaken piece of disconnected dirt."

The other guy replied, "Cheer up. There is no need to worry or fear. We will be found no later than next week. This coming Sunday is *Pledge the Budget Sunday* at my church and the Stewardship Committee will start looking for me on Monday."

Do you feel that the church comes looking for you at least once a year? Whether or not your congregation asks you and other members to make a financial pledge or commitment to the budget of your church, you are aware that the ministry of the church requires financial support. Furthermore, you are aware that at least once each year financial stewardship becomes the primary topic of conversation in announcements, newsletters, Sunday School classes, committee meetings, and sermons from the pulpit. You may receive something in the mail or notice new theme posters hanging in the halls. You may feel that people are looking for you so thoroughly that you couldn't hide on a deserted island.

Your money and the church's ministry are forever intertwined. Financial stewardship is a subject that is important to talk about even if it makes some people feel awkward, tense, guilty, or embarrassed. How people value money reflects on how their parents handled money, reveals how they perceive money as part of their socio-cultural experience, and unveils dimensions of their spiritual life.

Money is not a bad thing. There is nothing wrong with money. There is nothing sinful about having money. The Scriptures are plain, though, about the way Christians are to relate to money.

Learning to give is an ongoing course of study in Jesus' school of discipleship. One of the things God reveals through the Scriptures is that there are reasons for giving. Your financial giving should be motivated by your commitment to Christ and the mission of God. Helping people understand this idea when they are financially privileged is a real struggle sometimes, however. This is what Paul was finding out and speaking to in 2 Corinthians 8—9.

2 Corinthians 8:1–21

[1]And now, brothers, we want you to know about the grace that God has given the Macedonian churches. [2]Out of the most severe trial, their overflowing joy and their extreme poverty welled up in rich generosity. [3]For I testify that they gave as much as they were able, and even beyond their ability. Entirely on their own, [4]they urgently pleaded with us for the privilege of sharing in this service to the saints. [5]And they did not do as we expected, but they gave themselves first to the Lord and then to us in keeping with God's will. [6]So we urged Titus, since he had earlier made a beginning, to bring also to completion this act of grace on your part. [7]But just as you excel in everything—in faith, in speech, in knowledge, in complete earnestness and in your love for us—see that you also excel in this grace of giving.

[8]I am not commanding you, but I want to test the sincerity of your love by comparing it with the earnestness of others. [9]For you know the grace of our Lord Jesus Christ, that though he was rich, yet for your sakes he became poor, so that you through his poverty might become rich.

[10]And here is my advice about what is best for you in this matter: Last year you were the first not only to give but also to have the desire to do so. [11]Now finish the work, so that your eager willingness to do it may be matched by your completion of it, according to your means. [12]For if the willingness is there, the gift is acceptable according to what one has, not according to what he does not have.

[13]Our desire is not that others might be relieved while you are hard pressed, but that there might be equality. [14]At the present time your plenty will supply what they need, so that in turn their plenty will supply what you need. Then there will be equality, [15]as it is written: "He who gathered much did not have too much, and he who gathered little did not have too little."

[16]I thank God, who put into the heart of Titus the same concern I have for you. [17]For Titus not only welcomed our appeal, but he is coming to you with much enthusiasm and on his own initiative. [18]And we are sending along with him the brother who is praised by all the churches for his service to the gospel. [19]What is more, he was chosen by the churches to accompany us as we carry the offering, which we administer in order to honor the Lord himself and to show our eagerness to help. [20]We want to avoid any criticism of the way we administer this liberal gift. [21]For we are taking pains to do what is right, not only in the eyes of the Lord but also in the eyes of men.

An Inspiring Story of Giving (8:1–5)

Corinth was a wealthy city. Most likely, the believers in Corinth had more than plenty. Paul approached the young church in Corinth as a parent

Your money and the church's ministry are forever intertwined.

might approach a young child who is reluctant to share any toys in the toy box with a child who has no toys. The Corinthians were emotionally attached to their material possessions. Paul did not want to make them immediately defensive by requesting an offering for the needs of the Christians in Jerusalem. So Paul approached them with an inspiring story of giving. You might say that he told them about a child who did not have many toys but who asked to share with the child who had no toys.

Paul told the Corinthians how inspired he was by the churches of Macedonia. Paul was asking the Corinthians to value the needs of others above their desires to build wealth. This tension between Paul and the believers in and around Corinth presents a problem for Christians in the Western world. By one estimate, if the world were a global village of one hundred residents, six of them would be Americans. These six Americans would have half of the village's income. The other ninety-four residents would exist on the other half.[1]

In my community, this is the day after a catastrophe. A local family lost their home and all their possessions in an electrical fire yesterday. It was inspiring to see how people responded to their needs. Especially inspiring were some of those who gave. Some of those who were the first to give did not have the greatest ability to give. Actually, a few of those who responded immediately were *unable* to make contributions—but they did! They just stepped forward and gave of themselves, several of them sacrificially.

This was the story of the Macedonian church. The Macedonians inspired Paul. He wanted the Corinthians to know of their graciousness. He told of how he was inspired by the Macedonian churches in Berea, Thessalonica, and Philippi. Luke records how Paul was introduced to Macedonia in Acts 16—17. Paul had a vision during the night of a man from Macedonia standing and begging him, "Come over to Macedonia and help us" (Acts 16:9). Paul went to the leading city of that district of Macedonia; a city that was a Roman colony, Philippi.

Ministry Through the Baptist World Alliance

Far-reaching new approaches are possible as Baptists around the world cooperate in the mission of God. In our global village society, Denton Lotz, general secretary of the Baptist World Alliance (BWA), has called for a new global mission agency allowing Baptists from around the world to send and support missionaries from economically developing nations in the Third World—Asia, Africa, and Latin America. In May of 2003, Baptist leaders from 60 countries gathered in England for a weeklong *Global Summit on Baptist Mission in the 21st Century*. These Baptist leaders called for a new approach to sharing resources that supports the stated goals of the Baptist World Alliance: to unite Baptists worldwide, lead in world evangelization, respond to people in need, and defend human rights.

Christians of the Third World are responding to the call to serve in the mission of God among all the peoples of the world. Yet the churches of the Third World lack the financial resources to send and support their work. Formed in 1905, the Baptist World Alliance consists of 206 Baptist fellowships, unions, and conventions with a combined membership of more than 47 million baptized believers.[2]

It is possible that the Christian believers in Macedonia were in need of financial help themselves because they were being persecuted for their newfound faith. Macedonia, the ancient land of Alexander the Great, was the primary land route connecting Asia and Rome. Rome had used Macedonia, especially Philippi, as a settlement area for discharged military veterans. The inhabitants were granted Roman citizenship with all its rights and privileges. Few Jews lived in Macedonia. In fact, when Paul arrived in Philippi, there was no synagogue. After Paul and Silas were freed from jail in Philippi for healing a slave-girl fortune-teller, they went to Thessalonica. There was a synagogue in Thessalonica, but the Jews in charge of religiosity in town rounded up some bad characters, formed a mob, and started a riot in the city, blaming the believers for the trouble (Acts 17:1–9). Paul and Silas had to go to Berea. But, when the troublemakers in Thessalonica heard Paul and Silas had gone to Berea, they also traveled there to agitate the crowds and stir them up. It is easy to surmise that believers in Christ were not as well received in Macedonia as they were in the cosmopolitan and pluralistic Corinth.

These Macedonian churches, persecuted and less financially able than the Corinthian believers, had responded to God's grace in a wonderful way (2 Cor. 8:1). They were experiencing severe trials. Even so, their joy overflowed, bubbling up in rich generosity (8:2). They gave more than they were really able to give (8:3). Entirely at their own initiative, they urgently pleaded with Silas and Paul for the privilege of sharing in this offering to be given to the believers back in Jerusalem (8:4). Paul used an interesting phrase here: "the privilege of sharing" (8:4). As you learn to give, you learn that life is truly more blessed as you focus on giving rather than receiving.

The fund for needy Christians in Jerusalem assisted those who were some of the first to believe. The need to take care of the poor believers in Jerusalem first appears in Acts 6. The offering for the believers in Jerusalem continued for several years (Acts 24:17). There is something unique about being part of an offering that connects you with Christian people around the world and over time. Among the boundaries this offering crossed were geography, culture, and doctrinal belief.

Paul and Silas had some expectations as to how the Macedonian churches would participate in this offering. But these believers surprised Paul and Silas. The Macedonian churches inspired and humbled these two men by first and foremost giving themselves to God and then to Paul and Silas. These persecuted and impoverished believers renewed their priority commitment to God and then affirmed

Learning to give is an ongoing course of study in Jesus' school of discipleship.

their partnership with and trust in their friends according to the will of God (8:5).

By considering the Macedonian's example, you are learning to give. You are seeing reasons for giving. You are realizing that one of the compelling reasons for giving is to respond to the needs of others.

In addition, another reason to give is to follow the example of those who, despite their persecution and poverty, give themselves to God and to others from meager resources. By supporting the impoverished believers in Jerusalem, these Macedonians were part of something larger than themselves. They also expressed their belief that the suffering Christ did not see his suffering as an excuse for not giving of himself. Paul expressed his conviction that the primary reason the Macedonians were so willing to give was that they allowed the grace of God to work in them.

Finishing What You Begin (8:6–15)

In July of 2003, Lance Armstrong of Texas won the Tour de France a record-tying fifth time. Of course, he was favored to win again. Still, he won only because he finished.

After Paul informed the Corinthian church of the Macedonians' gracious and inspiring participation, he turned his attention to last year's conversation. Basically, Paul had written to the Corinthians in a previous letter about his desire for them to participate in this "collection for God's people," and they had responded (1 Cor. 16:1–4; see 2 Cor. 8:10). One year earlier, Paul had encouraged them to set aside an amount each week for this purpose and said that he would pick it up as he passed through after he traveled through Macedonia. Now he was sending Titus, who probably delivered the original letter to them, to complete the work. Paul affirmed the Corinthians for being a people who excelled in everything—in faith, in speech, in knowledge, in sincerity, and in their love for Paul and Titus. Then, as though he were an experienced fund-raiser writing a United Way brochure, he delivered his punch line: "see that you also excel in this grace of giving" (8:7).

As you learn to give, you learn that life is truly more blessed as you focus on giving rather than receiving.

Imagine you are one of the Corinthian believers huddled together listening to Titus or one of the leaders of the believing community as these words of Paul are read. After you hear that punch line, as a free citizen of Corinth and a child of God with plenty of toys in your toy box, you might

Facts to Consider

According to a recent estimate:

- Today's three-car garage is about 900 square feet. This compares in size to the average-size home in the 1950s.
- The income disparity between the rich and poor is greatest in the United States.
- Since 1950, Americans alone have used more natural resources than everyone who ever lived before them.
- Americans throw away seven million cars a year, two million plastic bottles an hour, and enough aluminum cans annually to make six thousand DC–10 airplanes.[3]

be thinking, *Wait just a minute, Paul. You said that the Macedonians begged to participate of their own volition. Don't start ordering us what to do.*

Then, the letter continues and you hear these words, "I am not commanding you, but I want to test the sincerity of your love by comparing it with the earnestness of others. For you know the grace of our Lord Jesus Christ, that though he was rich, yet for your sakes he became poor, so that you through his poverty might become rich" (8:8–9). Paul has now affirmed you, challenged you, and held Christ up to you as the one for you to follow. You are already in check and now Paul makes his next move for checkmate. You continue to listen to the reader of the letter and you hear, "Last year you were the first not only to give but also to have the desire to do so. Now finish the work, so that your eager willingness to do it may be matched by your completion of it, according to your means" (8:10–11).

> . . . The primary reason the Macedonians were so willing to give was that they allowed the grace of God to work in them.

I heard of a pastor who received a phone call one afternoon from an IRS agent. "Pastor, I am calling you to verify that Mr. Gary Walden has given $50,000 to your church." The quick-witted pastor replied, "Ma'am, I promise you that if he hasn't, he will."

Paul encouraged the Corinthian believers to have the willingness to finalize the gift so the gift was acceptable. He challenged them to give to help these other people according to what they had. There was no desire to simply invert the names and addresses of those who had relief and those who were hard pressed. What Paul was after was fairness. The believers in Jerusalem had the gospel and sent it your way. You have some financial resources to assist them and you should send them their way (8:12–15).

Assuring Financial Accountability (8:16–21)

Some people raise their defense shields the moment the preacher mentions money. In part, this is understandable. Hucksters, shysters, crooks, and thieves have been hanging around the Christian faith since Judas sold the Son of God for the price of a slave. But, ninety-nine percent of all congregations and pastors are quite responsible in their use of the monies given to the Lord for ministry.

You will remember there had been some conflict between Paul and the Corinthian church. The words of the correspondence we know as

1 Corinthians were not well received. Paul then made a "painful visit" to Corinth but decided to write rather than making another such visit (2 Cor. 2:1–3). Neither the letter nor the visit seemed to quiet the conflict. In our next unit of study, we will consider 2 Corinthians 10—13, which addresses this conflict. So, Paul was aware of this conflict as he challenged the Corinthians to contribute to the cause. This may explain why Titus and some others were picking up the offering. This may also explain why Paul was so inclined to explain that the money would be handled with accountability.

> *Maturing disciples of Jesus Christ grow in their willingness to live sacrificially in order to minister to the needs of other people.*

Their love offering for the poor in Jerusalem was to be placed in the hands of trustworthy people who were held in high esteem. In fact, one man was chosen by the churches to accompany Paul and Titus on this mission. Paul, Titus, and the others would go to any measure to avoid criticism for the way they handled this liberal gift of compassion (8:20–21). Their desire was to be pleasing to the eyes of the Lord. So they set policies, procedures, and practices in place to be above reproach.

Implications for Today

As you follow Jesus Christ, you take on his character and spirit. You are moved with compassion more and more. Maturing disciples of Jesus Christ grow in their willingness to live sacrificially in order to minister to the needs of other people.

Have you learned how to be a giving person? Unless you learn how to be a giving person, how can you be an obedient follower of Jesus Christ? When you begin taking ministry personally, by being the presence of Christ to others, you begin to live sacrificially. To follow Christ is to ask yourself continually: *Am I willing to will God's will in my life?*

QUESTIONS

1. Do you think your church talks too much about money? Does your church ask members to make pledges or commitments to the annual ministry budget? Why or why not?

2. Why do you think you are inspired when persecuted and impoverished people are gracious in their giving?

3. Do you believe it is possible to be a follower of Jesus Christ without being a giving person?

4. How many reasons for giving can you identify from today's lesson?

5. In what ways does growth as a giving person give evidence of the grace of God at work within that person?

6. Do you believe Christians in North America have a greater responsibility to express faithful financial stewardship toward the needs of others than do believers in developing nations?

NOTES

1. Donald E. Messer, *Contemporary Images of Christian Ministry* (Nashville: Abingdon Press, 1989), 175.
2. For information about the Baptist World Alliance, see *www.bwanet.org*.
3. *Affluenza*, a television production of KCTS/Seattle and Oregon Public Broadcasting. See *http://www.pbs.org/kcts/affluenza/diag/what.html*.

Focal Text

2 Corinthians 9:6–15

Background

2 Corinthians 9

Main Idea

God blesses us abundantly when we give.

Question to Explore

Is it really more blessed to give?

Study Aim

To describe blessings God provides when we give

Study and Action Emphases

- Affirm the Bible as our authoritative guide for life and ministry
- Develop a growing, vibrant faith
- Obey and serve Jesus by meeting physical, spiritual, and emotional needs
- Equip people for servant leadership

LESSON TEN

Blessings of Giving

Quick Read

As you become more like Jesus Christ, taking ministry personally, you will become more aware of the many ways God blesses you through your giving.

Mack and Stephanie Donaldson became convinced, through the conviction of the Holy Spirit of God, to tithe. They explained how for several years God brought the issue of money to their attention, and they just ignored it. They never had tithed and did not see how they would ever be able to afford to do so. In fact, the two or three percent they planned to give often disappeared before the offering plate passed on Sunday. They gave to the mission of God through their church, but not anywhere close to ten percent of their income. Neither of their families had a history of tithing. Rather, they gave what they had left over after financing their comfortable lifestyle and keeping multiple revolving credit cards afloat.

Mack and Stephanie were in serious debt. They just couldn't get away from the fact that God was calling them to focus on financial stewardship, though. They asked their pastor to suggest a workbook they could study on the subject. They looked at several resources before they selected *Christians and Money: A Guide to Personal Finance.*[1]

Through their study and discussion of Scripture and this resource, they wrote down three principles to which they committed themselves for the rest of their lives:

1. All of the money is God's, not ours. We are only trustees or stewards.
2. Unnecessary debt (beyond education, mortgage, and automobiles) makes us servants to money and forces us to serve two masters. Yet, we cannot serve money and the Lord.
3. We are to honor God with the firstfruits of our labors, not our leftovers.

While the Donaldsons could not twitch their noses and get out of debt, they sensed a direction from God that they should set aside the first ten percent of their income each month, giving five percent to the mission of God through the ministry budget of their church and using the other five percent to reduce their debt. They sensed that if they would follow this plan for four years, they would be out of debt and able to give the full ten percent through their church. While some people would probably criticize them for this plan, they felt peace about it between them and God. If they did not follow this plan, they might never quit serving their debt.

Three years and two months later (ten months ahead of schedule), they were debt free except for their mortgage, automobiles, and education loans. The next Sunday, they felt so blessed that they were able to give a full tithe to support the mission of God through their church. That was six years ago. Today, the Donaldsons give almost fifteen percent of their income to the mission of God each year. The blessings they receive from being able to give in this way are too numerous to count. Stephanie told her sister, "My life is completely transformed because I am able to focus on the needs of others instead of my burdens."

2 Corinthians 9:6–15

[6]Remember this: Whoever sows sparingly will also reap sparingly, and whoever sows generously will also reap generously. [7]Each man should give what he has decided in his heart to give, not reluctantly or under compulsion, for God loves a cheerful giver. [8]And God is able to make all grace abound to you, so that in all things at all times, having all that you need, you will abound in every good work. [9]As it is written:
   "He has scattered abroad his gifts to the poor;
   his righteousness endures forever."
[10]Now he who supplies seed to the sower and bread for food will also supply and increase your store of seed and will enlarge the harvest of your righteousness. [11]You will be made rich in every way so that you can be generous on every occasion, and through us your generosity will result in thanksgiving to God.
   [12]This service that you perform is not only supplying the needs of God's people but is also overflowing in many expressions of thanks to God. [13]Because of the service by which you have proved yourselves, men will praise God for the obedience that accompanies your confession of the gospel of Christ, and for your generosity in sharing with them and with everyone else. [14]And in their prayers for you their hearts will go out to you, because of the surpassing grace God has given you. [15]Thanks be to God for his indescribable gift!

Some Facts Worth Remembering (9:6–7)

Every document in the New Testament is written to a person or a congregation involved in the mission of God for the world. In 2 Corinthians, Paul was not telling the Christians to get involved in the mission of God. They had no choice about that. They understood that God's mission, revealed in Jesus Christ, had now been given to the church, the called-out followers of Christ.

But the Christians in Corinth did need to be reminded and challenged about the depth of their commitment and the breadth of their faithfulness to live as witnesses of Jesus Christ. Paul confronted them to translate their commitment to Christ and the mission of God into faithful lifestyle choices that showed up in their attitudes, decisions, and actions.

The stewardship of financial resources is one dimension of the Christian's spiritual life.

The fact is that if you invest only a little commitment and faithfulness in the kingdom of God, you will receive only a small return on your investment. A modern cliché is, "You get out of it what you put into it." This is not always true on Wall Street. There are some people who have made a bundle with a small investment. There are also some who have lost everything after making large investments. Paul teaches that things are different in the kingdom of God.

In 9:6, Paul was not suggesting that your financial portfolio is dependent on how much money you give to support the mission of God. His use of the agrarian metaphor of sowing and reaping was meant to show a spiritual truth, not an economic one. Yet, the truth spills over into financial stewardship as a reflection of spiritual commitment and faithfulness. The stewardship of financial resources is one dimension of the Christian's spiritual life.

In 9:7, Paul offered another truth to the Corinthian Christians. Baptist Christians have no difficulty with this verse because it is rooted in a principle we believe and promote called the soul competency of every believer.

They never had tithed and did not see how they would ever be able to afford to do so.

Paul said, "Each person should give what he has decided in his heart to give, not reluctantly or under compulsion, for God loves a cheerful giver."

The amount you give flows from your heart. The amount you give should not originate in a legalistic interpretation of Scripture. The amount you give should not originate in servitude to some family legacy or reputation. The amount you give should not be motivated by anything that creates resentment or negativity inside of you. When you write a check to insert into your giving envelope and place it in the offering plate on Sunday, you should not have any feeling of reluctance or sense that someone or something is forcing you to give that amount. You should decide in your heart what you should give, and you should be at peace about it.

But you should always ask yourself whether Christ is in full control of your heart. The Hebrew people, the people who wrote most of the Bible, understood the heart to be the center of the human life. According to the biblical perspective, your intentions, attitudes, morality, priorities, decisions, commitments, values, conscience, goals, principles, and habits are reflections of your heart. Your heart reflects your character—and the lack of

The amount you give flows from your heart.

it. Your heart expresses your integrity—and the gaps in it. If Christ is in full control of your heart and you decide in your heart what you should give (9:7), you will be cheerful about your decision. Paul proclaimed that God loves cheerful givers. While God may also love boisterous givers, resentful givers, and manipulative givers, these people's lives do not suggest that they experience the love of God in their hearts.

In these two verses of Scripture are three facts to remember (9:6–7):

1. *There is a relationship between sowing and reaping* What you harvest as joy, fulfillment, peace, hope, wisdom, character, understanding, grace, faith, etc., in the kingdom of God, is directly related to how you sow seeds of commitment and faithfulness.

2. *God has created you to be competent to decide what you should give.* You should give financial offerings only according to your heart and never give any financial offering to support the mission of God through your church that you are reluctant to give or because you feel pressured by some external force.

3. *Your heart should be formed by Christ so you experience "cheerful giver" status.* Your relationship with Christ should always be maturing in your heart so that you experience an increase in harvesting the blessings of a giving lifestyle.

The Economy of God's Grace (9:8–11)

You will be equipped to understand these verses better by considering verses 8:16–9:5. There had been some conflict between Paul and the Corinthian church. Many of the words of the correspondence we know as 1 Corinthians were not well received. Paul then made a "painful visit" to Corinth (2 Corinthians 2:1–9). However, the visit did not seem to quiet the conflict. Paul, aware of this conflict, sent Titus and two other unnamed highly esteemed and trustworthy men of integrity to Corinth to prepare the Corinthians (8:16–22). Then the Corinthians would be ready for their offering for the suffering believers in Jerusalem to be picked up (9:4).

While Paul had encouraged generosity among the Corinthians by citing the inspiring example of the impoverished and persecuted Macedonians, Paul had also encouraged the Macedonians by the deep commitment of the Corinthians one year earlier. Paul bragged on one church to another church (9:1–5). Paul had used the enthusiastic commitment of the Corinthians as an example when speaking among the churches of Macedonia. Paul said it would be a shame if the rich Corinthians did not follow through on their commitment of last year. This would mean his boasting words about them and their commitments were hollow.

The deep sense of human and spiritual community that occurs when a person says thank you through tears of joy and gratitude is indescribable.

In 9:8–11, we find Paul reminding the Corinthians that God's grace was the source of their giving. Just as the gracious initiative of the Macedonian participation in the offering did not depend on the depth of their resource base, the capacity of the Corinthians to give was not dependent on their resources. Their capacity to give was based on the abundant grace of God. Paul emphasized the complete sufficiency of God's grace by repeating the idea over and over in these verses. Paul used words of sufficiency such as "able," "all," "abound," and "every": "God is able;" "all grace;" "in all things;" "at all times;" "all you need;" "you will abound in every good work."

God's grace was sufficient as it supplied for their needs. Their gifts of grace on behalf of the needs of those in Jerusalem were simply scattering the seed of God's grace. Quoting Psalm 112:9, Paul strengthened his position by contrasting this person who scatters abroad with the one who sows sparingly (9:6). The economy of God's grace works as God supplies seed and bread. As the Corinthians gave to meet the needs of others, God enlarged the harvest of their righteousness.

When you give to meet the needs of someone else, the all-sufficient grace of God is at work in you and through you. You are not giving out of your own pantry of plenty. You are reaching into the cupboard of God's grace. One of the blessings of giving is to know you are participating in

Giving Through Reaching Out

Each summer, one Baptist congregation reaches out to its community in a way based on a theological perspective that the people of God must take ministry personally. During June, members of the congregation go out two by two to the homes in the area, asking one question: *Do you know of any ministry needs on your street?*

An informational listing of each congregation in the neighborhood is left with residents if they do not have a church home or if they do not answer the door. The list includes Baptist, Catholic, Episcopalian, Methodist, and Presbyterian churches. The list of needs gathered during the month is then compiled and assigned to ministry teams in the church for follow-up.

This practice affirms the Baptist principle that every Christian is a minister. It also fosters a giving spirit among the congregation and transcends the idea among unchurched people of the community that churches are just interested in getting money. The result is that the blessings of giving are released in the world.

---

the economy of God's grace. Another blessing of giving is having the righteousness of God as an enlarged harvest in your heart. As you learn to give, the character of Jesus Christ increases in your character, like a field yielding an increased harvest. Over time, you will become so spiritually rich in the character of Christ that in every way, you can be a generous giving person on every occasion.

> . . . You should always ask yourself whether Christ is in full control of your heart.

God's Economic Cycle (9:12–15)

As you take ministry personally, you learn to give. Then, as you learn to give, you experience the blessings of giving.

One of the blessings of giving is that you are involved in meeting the needs of God's people (9:12). While Paul was referring here to the impoverished Christians in Jerusalem, every person is a creation of God. As you know, there are many ways to give in addition to financial giving. You give to another person by remembering the anniversary of a death and calling to let the person know you are praying for him or her that day. You give

103

to another person by forgiving the person. You give to another person by listening without judging. As you learn to be a giving person, you begin to forget how to be a craving person. You begin to focus more on giving of yourself to meet the needs of others rather than fixating on getting your needs met. In fact, getting your mind off of yourself is another blessing of giving.

Once you get to the point where you desire for people to praise God rather than you for an act of generosity, you experience a new dimension of the blessings of giving.

Another blessing of giving is that people give thanks to God for their needs being met (9:12). While someone may say *thank you* to you, they also express their thanks to God, the Giver behind all givers and all gifts.

In addition to thanking God, people will also praise God because you were obedient in your commitment to be like Christ in spirit, character, and behavior (9:13). They will praise God for your generosity. Once you get to the point where you desire for people to praise God rather than you

Reasons for Giving, Barriers to Giving

It has been suggested that people give to support the mission of God through their church for one or more of the following reasons:
- Opportunity giving—responding to a special need
- Organizational giving—supporting the budget
- Obedient giving—responding to Scriptural teachings
- Ordained giving—setting apart gifts based on God's leadership

Which of these best reflects your motive to give?

The following list offers some barriers to giving. Can you name others?
- Greed
- Cultural expectation
- Ignorance
- Fear
- Selfishness
- Rigidity
- Narrow-mindedness
- Lack of awareness

for an act of generosity, you experience a new dimension of the blessings of giving.

Then, because of your generous acts of giving, people will extend their hearts to you (9:14). I can still see her face. She stood on the porch of her new house provided through volunteer labor by a congregation of Christians and Habitat for Humanity. The deep sense of human and spiritual community that occurs when a person says *thank you* through tears of joy and gratitude is indescribable. You just have to learn to become a giving person to experience that blessing of giving. Yet, it is a mere reflection of the joy and gratitude we express to God for the indescribable gift of Jesus Christ (9:15).

> *If you sow generously the grace of God, you will find the heart of Christ being formed in you and the character of Christ increasing in you.*

Implications for Today

There are many blessings of giving. It is a fact that unless you sow generously the grace of God toward the needs of others, you will not reap the blessings of giving. If you sow generously the grace of God, you will find the heart of Christ being formed in you and the character of Christ increasing in you. So, if you learn to give, you will

- understand God's grace more and more
- be used of God to meet the needs of others
- get your mind off yourself
- enable other people to express their thanks and praise to God
- experience a sense of human and spiritual community that is indescribable

As you experience the blessings of giving, your life will express your thanks and praise to God for the indescribable gift of your Lord and Savior, Jesus Christ, who became poor for your sake and gave it all.

QUESTIONS

1. What do you think about the situation of Mack and Stephanie Donaldson? Do you understand their situation? What do you think about the way they approached their spiritual challenge?

2. Paul instructed that each and every believer should decide in his or her own heart what to give. Does this apply only to love offerings to alleviate the needs of others or does this also apply to whether a Christian tithes?

3. Is it important for Christians to increase in their percentage of giving to support the mission of God through their church? Why or why not?

4. Can you give an example of how the blessings of giving have been a reality in your life or in the life of your church?

5. Do you think your church focuses more of its energy on giving to others or does it focus most of its energy on meeting its own institutional and organizational needs? Give examples to support your answer.

NOTES

1. Don W. Joiner, *Christians and Money: A Guide to Personal Finance* (Discipleship Resources: Nashville, Tennessee, 1991).

Getting Beyond the Status Quo

Many churches get confused and conflicted along the way. Some churches who have had wonderful days in years past try to duplicate the programs, structures, and initiatives that made such a solid impact back then. Other congregations compare themselves with churches larger than their membership and try to replicate their styles, approaches, charismatic leaders, facilities, etc. They are trying to improve themselves; they are seeking to get beyond the status quo. But, unless they are careful, they may be like the person who climbed to the top rung of the ladder of success only to find the ladder was leaning against the wrong wall.

When Jesus Christ commissioned his followers to teach all people groups of the world as they went about their daily living (Matthew 28:18–20), Jesus established the only status quo worth our efforts. Jesus wants his church, his called-out people, to join him in his mission. Jesus sends us forth on the mission of immersing new followers in a relationship with God by teaching them to obey everything Jesus taught. Anything less than this mission is below Jesus' expectation.

Along the way, as we fulfill the commission of Christ, we may get confused and conflicted as we learn to deal with authority, resources, and one another. This reality was present in the church of Corinth and lies in the background of 2 Corinthians 10—13. If, however, we involve ourselves in the mission of God through the Spirit of Christ, we will get beyond the status quo of our church's history or the performance of another church. If we involve ourselves in the mission of God through the Spirit of Christ, we will begin measuring up to the status quo of our Lord.[1]

UNIT THREE, GETTING BEYOND THE STATUS QUO

NOTES

1. Unless otherwise indicated, all Scripture quotations in unit three are from The Holy Bible, New International Version (North American Edition), copyright © 1973, 1978, 1984 by the International Bible Society. Used by permission of Zondervan Publishing House.

Focal Text

2 Corinthians 10

Background

2 Corinthians 10

Main Idea

Dealing positively with conflict in the church calls for mutual respect, positive motives, clear communication, accurate information, and a shared commitment to the Lord.

Question to Explore

How can church conflicts be solved or prevented?

Study Aim

To identify positive ways of dealing with church conflicts and state implications for current church life

Study and Action Emphases

- Affirm the Bible as our authoritative guide for life and ministry
- Develop a growing, vibrant faith
- Include all God's family in decision-making and service
- Value all people as created in the image of God
- Equip people for servant leadership

LESSON ELEVEN

Dealing with Conflict

Quick Read

When you take ministry personally, you will find yourself dealing with conflict because you are determined to get beyond the status quo.

Nobody goes to church because they like to fight—well, almost nobody. Oh sure, there are disagreements over moving classrooms, color of the choir robes, selection of hymns, length of sermons, Wednesday night menus, procedures, budgets, personnel, location of the handicapped parking spots, social and racial diversity, and the sound system. But, for the most part, people in the church get along with one another.

We all hate to hear of churches in conflict. Even if it is a congregation of another denomination in another city, we find ourselves feeling a little sad when we learn about a church that is in the middle of a struggle. These struggles may be due to contradicting perspectives, extreme theological diversity, interpersonal differences, moral failure, or arguments over the use (misuse, abuse) of influence, authority, and power by leadership. There are several excellent resources to help you understand causes of and negotiate passages through church conflict. A list is given in this lesson.

While we may not go looking for conflict at church, it is inevitable. A congregation consists of diverse individual members, and each member's perspective is valued. Yet, while each perspective is valued, every perspective cannot predominate in the life of the church. Compromise and consensus building are ongoing processes in congregational life. If differences go ignored for long periods of time, if one particular person or small group consistently dominates decision-making, if signs of internal stress are not addressed, then church conflict exists. This conflict eventually will find its way to the surface of congregational energy. Even when there are no easily detectible signs of conflict, conflict can exist below the surface. This hidden conflict may show itself as cynicism, blaming, keeping secrets, and manipulation. These are signs of an impending blowup, like smoke seeping from a volcano.

Sometimes the conflict that exists within a congregation has to be confronted. The spirit in which the conflict is approached is significant. The outcome of the conflict is less important than the way in which the conflict is handled by the congregational leadership.

Throughout my thirty years of pastoral ministry, there have been occasions when the attitudes, words, and actions of people have demanded confrontation. When individuals or groups are causing injury to another person or damage to the health of the church, then they must be confronted. When individuals or groups are being motivated more by their own desires, pursuits, or needs—even if they are blind to their motivations—they must be confronted. In church life, dealing with conflict is necessary at times. Wise congregational leaders realize that resolving and managing conflict is an ongoing responsibility for them as they nurture the health and vitality of the church.

In 2 Corinthians 10, Paul had to confront some people who were sowing bad seed in the church. You might say some folks had entered the church and were attempting a hostile takeover through innuendo, lies, and character assaults. Paul approached the situation as a pastoral servant, not as a heavy-handed tyrant. For Paul, authority had more to do with a basin and towel than it did with an anvil and hammer. He desired reconciliation and healing, not ridicule and pain.

2 Corinthians 10

[1]By the meekness and gentleness of Christ, I appeal to you—I, Paul, who am "timid" when face to face with you, but "bold" when away! [2]I beg you that when I come I may not have to be as bold as I expect to be toward some people who think that we live by the standards of this world. [3]For though we live in the world, we do not wage war as the world does. [4]The weapons we fight with are not the weapons of the world. On the contrary, they have divine power to demolish strongholds. [5]We demolish arguments and every pretension that sets itself up against the knowledge of God, and we take captive every thought to make it obedient to Christ. [6]And we will be ready to punish every act of disobedience, once your obedience is complete.

[7]You are looking only on the surface of things. If anyone is confident that he belongs to Christ, he should consider again that we belong to Christ just as much as he. [8]For even if I boast somewhat freely about the authority the Lord gave us for building you up rather than pulling you down, I will not be ashamed of it. [9]I do not want to seem to be trying to frighten you with my letters. [10]For some say, "His letters are weighty and forceful, but in person he is unimpressive and his speaking amounts to nothing." [11]Such people should realize that what we are in our letters when we are absent, we will be in our actions when we are present.

[12]We do not dare to classify or compare ourselves with some who commend themselves. When they measure themselves by themselves and compare themselves with themselves, they are not wise. [13]We, however, will not boast beyond proper limits, but will confine our boasting to the field God has assigned to us, a field that reaches even to you. [14]We are not going too far in our boasting, as would be the case if we had not come to you, for we did get as far as you with the gospel of Christ. [15]Neither do we go beyond our limits by boasting of work done by others. Our hope is that, as your faith continues to grow, our area of activity among you will

greatly expand, [16]so that we can preach the gospel in the regions beyond you. For we do not want to boast about work already done in another man's territory. [17]But, "Let him who boasts boast in the Lord." [18]For it is not the one who commends himself who is approved, but the one whom the Lord commends.

When Authority Is Appealing (10:1–6)

The authority of Paul serves as an example for all church leaders for all time. He proposed that his authority was not rooted in the weapons of this world. Paul's weapons were meekness and gentleness (10:1–4). The way for a Christian to address the conflicts and wars of this world is through the characteristics of Jesus. The character of Christ carries us forward, with his cross going before us.

Chapters 10—13 may well be out of sequence in what we refer to as 2 Corinthians. We sit down to read a letter from the first word to the last word. But in my view 1 and 2 Corinthians is a collection of letters and letter fragments sent at different times to the church in Corinth. Chapters 10—13 of 2 Corinthians have been called "the anguished letter," because of Paul's reference in 2 Corinthians 2:3–4. The exact timing of this letter is unknown. But many biblical scholars propose it was sent prior to 2 Corinthians 1—9.

Nobody goes to church because they like to fight—well, almost nobody.

The letter fragment we have in 2 Corinthians 10—13 begins without Paul's usual greeting. Paul used words that jump right into the issues of conflict. Writing to the whole church in Corinth, Paul served as his own defense attorney responding to the accusations of some "super-apostles" who had moved in among the Corinthians (11:5). These self-appointed superstars were accusing Paul of being inferior to them. Evidently, Paul's detractors were boastful, charismatic, trained orators (10:12–18; 11:5–6). They accused Paul of being weak and timid when in Corinth but bold when he was absent from them using his pen and parchment (10:1, 9–10).

Authority is moot until it is activated. Some people activate their authority as a church leader by being gregarious and arrogant. Some people activate their authority by focusing on the power of their position. Others activate their authority through the influence of their personal Christian character. Paul's activation of authority was appealing to others because the Christ in them would respond to Christ in the leader.

Paul could have activated his authority with the Corinthians by focusing on his positional power in their lives—that is, his title. In contrast, Paul was enrolled in Jesus' finishing school of discipleship and character formation. Paul approached this conflict in Corinth through meekness. You get acquainted with meekness through humility, authenticity, honesty, and vulnerability. Paul also approached the Corinthians through

Your Church's Focus

One Baptist principle, the ministry of all the people of God, becomes confused when a pastor and congregation place leadership authority on the position of pastor, no matter whether the pastor exhibits the character of Christ in a situation. Is your church more pastor-focused or mission-focused? Which list best describes your congregation?[1]

Pastor-Focused Congregation

1. Excessive focus on pastor
2. Dependency-based; no activity unless the pastor is present
3. Neediness is fostered
4. Pastor is expected to motivate, uplift, or rescue people
5. A prescribed way of functioning
6. Pastor is "owned" by the congregation
7. No one confronts inappropriate behavior
8. Pastor views diversity as a threat
9. Disagreements are dangerous
10. Closed system; little or no feedback

Mission-Focused Congregation

1. A clear answer to the question why we are here now
2. Interdependence is encouraged
3. Needs met by many
4. Pastor expected to organize and equip people toward mission
5. A flexible way of functioning
6. Pastor is viewed as a separate self by the church
7. Lots of relational dialogue
8. Vision guides and bridges diversity
9. Conflict is normal and necessary
10. Open system; lots of feedback

gentleness. You get to know gentleness through sensitivity, grace, and charity. Notice that Paul did not try to be as meek and gentle as *he* could be. Rather, he sought to express the meekness and gentleness of *Christ*.

Christlike meekness and gentleness exercise divine power in conflict situations and in people's hearts to demolish the strongholds and walls set up by arguments and pretense (10:4–5). The meekness and gentleness of Christ takes captive every thought and brings it under submission to the One who was born in a stable, placed in a cattle trough as an infant, had no pillow for his head, made of himself no reputation, battled with a basin and towel, was killed on trumped-up charges, and was buried in a borrowed tomb. The meekness and gentleness of Christ, when activated in the character of the church leader, makes the authority of the leader appealing.

Wise congregational leaders realize that resolving and managing conflict is an ongoing responsibility for them as they nurture the health and vitality of the church.

Jesus said, "Come to me, all you who are weary and burdened, and I will give you rest. Take my yoke upon you and learn from me, for I am gentle and humble in heart, and you will find rest for your souls" (Matthew 11:28–29). Through the first eleven chapters of Matthew, Jesus called people to the kingdom of God and to repentance. In these verses, Jesus specifically called people to himself. Your desire to have a relationship with God is the reason Jesus came into the world. Jesus wants you to find rest for your soul. If you have never allowed all of your self to come to Jesus, please do so.

A professor gave the freshman college class an assignment. "Learn everything you can about an orange," the professor said. One group of students headed directly to the library. They learned such things as the molecular structure of the orange; the amount of vitamin C in an orange; the best soil and climatic conditions in which to grow oranges; the average size, weight, and edible content of an orange; and the thickness of the peel. They returned with knowledge of a variety of products in which oranges are used. Another group of students went to the library for the same research. But they first went to the produce section of a grocery store. These students bought oranges, peeled them, and ate them. The first group *knew about* the orange. The second group of students *knew* the orange.

So it is with your relationship with Jesus Christ. If you know Jesus, you want to learn from him, and you want to learn about him. The yoke

Authority

Authority includes the ability to influence decision-making in a congregation's life. Some people assume authority by virtue of their position. (These are the official "governors" of the congregation.) Some people are assigned authority because of their spirit and character. (These are the "E.F. Huttons" of the congregation. People respect them.) Some people acquire authority by the longevity of their tenure in the congregation. (These are the "owls" of the church.) Identify which group seems to have the most authority in your church.

of Jesus is humble obedience to the humble God made known in the humble Jesus.

A person was once asked whether he felt as though his personal freedom of thought was limited because of his commitment to Christ. "Actually," he said, "I am more free in my thinking because I am not limited by the philosophies or theories or knowledge or data or information that can be known by every other person. I am free to discover the hidden potential of my character that can only be known when my thoughts are expressed under submission to Christ."

Looking Below the Surface (10:7–11)

On the surface, these super-apostles were attractive to the church (10:7). But Paul went to the deeper characteristics of authoritative church leadership. If the Corinthian church gave authority to these people because of their oratorical ability, self-righteous self-assured selfishness, or braggadocio, the church would end up following a gospel other than the gospel delivered to them by Paul (see 11:1–4).

The way for a Christian to address the conflicts and wars of this world is through the characteristics of Jesus.

There is always a temptation to look only on the "surface of things" (10:7). Evidently these super-apostles were creating ways to determine who was a Christian and who was not. They were setting up criteria that provided confidence if a person's beliefs agreed with theirs, but not if a person's beliefs agreed with Paul. Notice Paul did not condemn or deny that his detractors were committed to Christ. He simply stated that he was committed to Christ.

Some Resources on the Subject of Church Conflict

Charles H. Cosgrove and Dennis D. Hatfield. *Church Conflict: The Hidden Systems Behind the Fights.* Nashville, Tennessee: Abingdon Press, 1994. (ISBN 0–687-08152–1)

Lloyd Edwards. *How We Belong, Fight, and Pray: The MBTI as a Key to Congregational Dynamics.* Bethesda, Maryland: Alban Institute, 1993. (ISBN 1–56699–114–5)

Larry L. McSwain and William C. Treadwell. *Conflict Ministry in the Church.* Nashville, Tennessee: Broadman Press, 1981. (ISBN 0–8054-2540–3)

George Parsons and Speed B. Leas. *Understanding Your Congregation As A System.* Bethesda, Maryland: Alban Institute, 1993. (ISBN 1–56699–118–8)

Peter Steinke. *Healthy Congregations: A Systems Approach.* Bethesda, Maryland: Alban Institute, 1996. (ISBN 1–56699–173-0)

Peter Steinke. *How Your Church Family Works: Understanding Congregations as Emotional Systems.* Bethesda, Maryland: Alban Institute, 1993. (ISBN 1–56699–110–2)[2]

One cannot determine whether a person is a faithful follower of Christ by looking on the surface. Signing one's name to some creedal or doctrinal document does not mean that one person's commitment to Christ has more integrity than another person's. Self-appointed superstars still show up in Christ's church to inflate their own importance and demonize those who do not have to rely on the power of position to have authority. Those guided by meekness and gentleness can be confident that they belong to Christ. They do not need the approval of those whose Christian practices beg people to focus only on the surface of reality.

Some people flatter themselves by comparing themselves to other people.

Church leaders whose authority lies below the surface in the influence of their character build up the spiritual lives of believers (10:8). The authority of church leaders who are self-appointed superstars is only surface-deep, residing in the influence of their position or their charisma. They have no spiritual power once they are removed from their positions. Because their motivations are self-serving, they actually pull down the spiritual lives of believers by creating structures based on fear, forced conformity, uniformity, and co-dependency (control by another).

Paul had no desire to use any of these approaches with the Corinthians. He did not even want to frighten them with the boldness of the words in his correspondence (10:9).

In 10:10–11, Paul was responding to the charges of that unnamed "some." These people always show up in church conflict. What seasoned church leader has not received at least one unsigned letter from a self-appointed accuser? In Corinth, "some" were saying that Paul was a strong writer and a weak speaker. "Some" accused Paul of being downright "unimpressive" in person. Imagine the Apostle Paul being told, *We would like to have you on our approved speaker's bureau list so we could encourage conference and seminar planners to invite you, but you just don't have what it takes.*

How wonderful it would be if every congregation of believers would have a vision to send the gospel beyond their own address.

Do you want your heart to be shaped by church leaders who reflect the character of Christ? Do you want to be nurtured in your spiritual life by people whose authority lies in the depths of their character? Then you will have to look below the surface.

The Lord's Seal of Approval (10:12–18)

Bill asked Charles, "How are you doing today?" Charles replied, "Compared to what?"

Some people flatter themselves by comparing themselves to other people. They rationalize, *Well, I'm a better Christian than old J.P.* Paul proclaimed this practice to be unwise (10:12). When you compare yourself to Christ, you see that you are not as good as you think you are. (For further understanding on Paul's idea, see Ephesians 4:11–16.)

Paul exemplified that it is better to just state the facts about yourself and let your record be your recommendation. Paul did not need to go around boasting about himself by comparing himself with others. But he could remind the Corinthians that he was the one who brought the gospel of Jesus Christ to them (10:13–14). His role in their lives was secure. He did not need to create stories and pretend them to be true (10:15a).

Paul's vision was for Corinth to be a mission-sending church. He hoped that, from Corinth, he could take the gospel to regions beyond them (10:15b–16). He would like to move on to Spain (see Romans 15:24–28).

How wonderful it would be if every congregation of believers would have a vision to send the gospel beyond their own address. In an age when so much congregational attention and energy is being given to beliefs, buildings, and budgets, it would be an act of God for churches to determine how they could help start new congregations.

Paul referred to Jeremiah 9:24 for the second time in his letters to Corinth (10:17–18; see also 1 Corinthians 1:31). Paul lived his life before an audience of One.

Implications for Us

If a church is ever going to get beyond the status quo of its own history or competition with other churches, the people must focus on Christ's mission for his church. Along the way, they may have to deal with some church conflicts.

In the midst of these conflicts, you and your church will have to determine who expresses the appealing characteristics of leadership authority by reflecting the spirit of Christ. You and your church will have to look below the surface of pretense that asks you to focus on loud talk, flashy personalities, and people who say, *Look at me.* You and your church will have to compare yourself with Jesus Christ and have a vision to take and send the gospel to regions beyond. If you will involve yourselves in the mission of God through the spirit of Christ, you will begin measuring up to the standard of our Lord.

Paul lived his life before an audience of One.

QUESTIONS

1. Have you been through a church conflict situation that was handled well? What contributed to this being so?

2. Who are some church leaders who express authority that is appealing because they exhibit the characteristics and spirit of Christ?

3. Why do you think some church leaders seem to be capable only of leading through arrogance and positional power?

4. How does the depth of maturity in a person's relationship with Christ affect how the person handles a church conflict situation? Why is it so important that church leaders be meek and gentle?

5. Does it seem to you there is an extraordinary number of self-aggrandizing leaders in today's church?

6. Where are some "regions beyond" (10:16) that your church should consider taking or sending the gospel? What are ways that your church is involved in starting new churches?

NOTES

1. Peter L. Steinke, *Healthy Congregations: a Systems Approach* (Bethesda, Maryland: Alban Institute, 1996), 44–45.
2. Listing a book does not imply full agreement by the writer or BAPTISTWAY PRESS® with all of its comments.

Focal Text

2 Corinthians 12:1–10

Background

2 Corinthians 11:1—12:13

Main Idea

Our strength is not in our accomplishments but in Christ.

Question to Explore

What is your greatest strength?

Study Aim

To summarize Paul's meaning in these verses and recall experiences in which I have found God's grace, not my strength, to be sufficient

Study and Action Emphases

• Affirm the Bible as our authoritative guide for life and ministry
• Develop a growing, vibrant faith
• Equip people for servant leadership

LESSON TWELVE

Grace Sufficient

Quick Read

As you take ministry personally, you will be determined to get beyond the status quo by relying more and more on God's grace and less and less on your strength.

"When a thorn pierces your foot, your whole body must bend over to pull it out." This Zulu proverb reminds us that while an infirmity may affect only one aspect of our lives, humility involves the whole person.

Her name was Carma Ann. She had three teenage sons. She and her husband Bill lived on a small farm where they grew enough hay to feed their six horses. Bill was director of human relations in a company located in the suburbs of the nearby city. The diagnosis was a shock. The doctor informed them that Carma Ann had multiple sclerosis. She had to quit teaching school. She suffered severely through the years. But she was a joy to know, and visits with her were opportunities to draw closer to Christ.

Carma Ann especially liked it when young children visited her. She liked to tell them stories. Those parents who took their children to visit during the years of Carma Ann's illness allowed their children to ask Carma Ann their honest questions about her feelings and thoughts. Mingled in her answers, she also talked about her walk with Jesus Christ.

Carma Ann tried to help Bill and the boys understand how much she loved them and appreciated their care for her. They were faithful to care for her as long as they could. Then they hired caregivers who came into their home each day. One of the boys went off to a university in a distant state and returned home twice a year. The other two entered military service and were stationed overseas. Bill said they couldn't watch her suffer anymore, and so they found noble ways to disappear.

Eventually, Carma Ann's care needs increased to the point that Bill placed her in a care facility. Bill's visits became more sporadic. He met a woman at the office and divorced Carma Ann to marry her. When she was asked whether she wanted to talk about Bill's departure from her life, all Carma Ann would say is, "I know who holds tomorrow, and I know who holds my hand." When Carma Ann died, her earthly possessions consisted of a hairbrush she could not hold, three books she could not read, and one Bible. But Carma Ann knew that life consists of so much more than earthly possessions.

You see, she had a recurring dream. She dreamed that when she was welcomed into the presence of Jesus Christ, there was Moses, Elijah, Jeremiah, Peter, and Paul. There was Ruth, Deborah, Mary Magdalene, and Mary the mother of Jesus. In her dream, when she entered the room, Christ stood and so did all the others. Then Carma Ann heard Jesus say something to her. She never told what he said. But she knew; she knew down deep within her spirit. She knew who holds tomorrow, and she knew who held her hand.

2 Corinthians 12:1–10

[1]I must go on boasting. Although there is nothing to be gained, I will go on to visions and revelations from the Lord. [2]I know a man in Christ who fourteen years ago was caught up to the third heaven. Whether it was in the body or out of the body I do not know—God knows. [3]And I know that this man—whether in the body or apart from the body I do not know, but God knows—[4]was caught up to paradise. He heard inexpressible things, things that man is not permitted to tell. [5]I will boast about a man like that, but I will not boast about myself, except about my weaknesses. [6]Even if I should choose to boast, I would not be a fool, because I would be speaking the truth. But I refrain, so no one will think more of me than is warranted by what I do or say.

[7]To keep me from becoming conceited because of these surpassingly great revelations, there was given me a thorn in my flesh, a messenger of Satan, to torment me. [8]Three times I pleaded with the Lord to take it away from me. [9]But he said to me, "My grace is sufficient for you, for my power is made perfect in weakness." Therefore I will boast all the more gladly about my weaknesses, so that Christ's power may rest on me. [10]That is why, for Christ's sake, I delight in weaknesses, in insults, in hardships, in persecutions, in difficulties. For when I am weak, then I am strong.

Visions and Revelations from the Lord (12:1)

Do you have a deep, abiding peace in your life? In your walk with Christ, is there an assurance within you that is calm and tranquil like a shimmering lake in a summer sunset? If you do not have this peace, have you ever known someone who does? No matter what external factors enter the person's life, whether divorce, disease, poverty, or abandonment by family, he or she remains calm due to the peace of God that passes understanding. This is the peace of God Paul knew (Philippians 4:4–9).

In the words of Gail Neal, "The Kingdom of God has no military to protect it, no international alliance to promote it, no commander-in-chief to lead it. Rather, members of this culture have faith that, regardless of external obstacles, communal persecution, personal hardship, or political legislation, the Kingdom of God will thrive only and always by the power of God through the Holy Spirit. Because it believes in the resurrection of the body to eternal life through Jesus Christ, this culture embodies absolute trust in spite of evidence to the contrary."[1]

One of the ways Paul came to experience this absolute trust is through "visions and revelations" (2 Corinthians 12:1). Absolute trust delivers to a person the peace of God. The peace of God becomes a staple of one's spiritual life as one allows himself or herself to experience the assurance of God. God offers assurance through visions and revelations.

"Visions" are mental pictures of God's truth. We might think of "revelations" as insights and *aha* moments that speak to our heart. "Visions and revelations" are sacred experiences that you do not describe without feeling like you are walking on holy ground.

> When Paul wrote to the church in Corinth, he challenged them to move beyond the status quo that occurs when people get caught up in living according to their own strength.

God enables you to experience assuring visions and revelations through promises kept and prophecies fulfilled. God assures you through your sense of agreement between your spirit and God's Holy Spirit. God provides you assurance through Scriptures that reveal God's heart and through nature that renews itself. God assures you and grants you peace through other people who are sent as answers to your prayers and to inspire you. But, most of all, God assures you through the resurrection of Jesus Christ from the dead. In Christ, God says to you, *The worst thing that could ever happen to you has already happened; and his grave is empty!*

Talking About Oneself (12:2–6)

A woman named Sara arrived at a dinner party and found her seat at a table with several friends. She knew everyone at the table except one person. She introduced herself, and the stranger told her his name. He then took off like a jetliner telling about himself, his accomplishments, and his position in the community. Sara was embarrassed for him, and she noticed several other people at the table seemed to share her sentiment. It has been said that the reason a dog is a human's best friend is because it wags its tail and not its tongue.

When Paul wrote to the church in Corinth, he challenged them to move beyond the status quo that occurs when people get caught up in living according to their own strength. When people live according to their own strength, one of the sins that takes over is pride. So, here was Paul desiring to take the Christians of Corinth to deeper waters, and the only boat he had to charter was his own. He wanted to get the people to focus on the truth of God, not on him, the absent apostle.

Paul had no Christian classics, song lyrics, or best-selling author to quote. He had no biographies or "Chicken Soup" stories to tell. All Paul had was his own experience, his own testimony. And he knew that if he kept writing about himself, the people would consider him to be boasting. The self-appointed super-apostles who had infiltrated the Corinthian church were *A*+ students in boasting. Paul had no desire to compete with them in this endeavor. But he did desire to enrich the lives of the Corinthians. He wanted to nurture their faith and trust and to equip them with the peaceful assurance of God, through God's Christ, the victorious Suffering Servant.

Paul regretted that he had to tell about his revelations and visions from the Lord, but it was what he had to tell. We are informed this is his own story by his reference in 12:7. He told his story as though he were a spectator in his own life.

The story Paul told is about a time, fourteen years earlier, when he "was caught up to the third heaven . . . to paradise" (12:2–3). We are given no specifics of this experience. All we know is that this experience in Paul's life was so memorable that he marked his life by it. Everything that happened in his life prior to that experience had to be reinterpreted through the hope, peace, and assurance of God.

If you have pleaded with the Lord to take away some burden or torment in your life, and your prayer has not been answered, you may want to consider how Paul interpreted his unanswered prayer.

Paul said he was caught up to "the third heaven." He lost touch with the concept of having a human body to the point that he did not know whether he was in his body or out of his body. All he knew was that it was "paradise." The idea of paradise comes from a Persian word meaning *a walled garden*. The image is of a secret garden, where everything is beautiful and well-tended, a place where all troubles can be left behind.

The Jews spoke of multiple heavens. Some believed in seven; most believed in three. The first heaven was the sky, where birds fly. The second heaven was space, where stars and planets orbit. The third heaven was paradise, where God dwells.

In John's Gospel, Jesus is quoted, "Do not let your hearts be troubled. Trust in God; trust also in me. In my Father's house are many rooms; if it were not so, I would have told you. I am going there to prepare a place for you. And if I go and prepare a place for you, I will come back and take you to be with me that you also may be where I am" (John 14:1–3).

In the Hebrew perspective, the heart is the center of the human life. Your reasoning, desiring, speaking, and behaving all emanate from your heart. As you study the teachings of Jesus, note that Jesus desires for your heart to be trusting, pure, humble, serving, forgiving, understanding, wise, and loving. Jesus also desires that your heart not be hardened, evil, doubtful, adulterous, or troubled. Jesus does not want your heart to be troubled about eternal life.

> *In your imagination, you can see Paul, with a glint in a friendly eye, asking for their forgiveness for never asking them to pay his bills.*

Jesus does not tell us where heaven is or exactly what happens in paradise. Jesus did tell the thief on the cross that he was taking him to paradise that day (Luke 23:43). If paradise is a good enough place for Jesus, it will be just fine. Jesus did say he did not want us to let our hearts be troubled about it.

When Paul wrote to the Corinthian church regarding his vision and revelation about paradise, he was making an effort to move them beyond their focus on "the surface of things" (10:7) and "foolishness" (11:1). He was encouraging them to focus on the grace of God. But he could not ask them to leap the chasm. He had to build a bridge for them to move beyond the status quo.

Unanswered Prayer

Prayers are not always answered *yes*. Sometimes, God answers a prayer *yes*, sometimes *no*, sometimes *wait*, and sometimes *your prayer has already been answered*.

Carrying physical and spiritual burdens can be like thorns sticking in our flesh or bitter cups that we must drink. Bowing in the Garden of Gethsemane, in complete humility, Jesus pleaded, "My Father, if it is possible, may this cup be taken from me. Yet, not as I will, but as you will" (Matthew 26:39). Then Jesus walked through the next day of betrayal, false accusations, beatings, embarrassment, ridicule, pain, suffering, agony, and death.

The Father did not answer Jesus' prayer the way Jesus willed. But the Father gave Jesus the grace sufficient to drink the cup. God's grace was sufficient to carry Jesus through the moments when he felt forsaken by God. God's grace was sufficient when Jesus committed his spirit to the Father. And God's grace was sufficient to cause an earthquake, send an angel, and raise Jesus from the dead.

Second Corinthians 11:1—12:13 has been called "The Fool's Speech." Paul knew that all this talk about himself, his experiences, his exploits, his travels, his beatings, his imprisonments, his endangerments, his hunger, and his pressures as a church leader was mere foolishness. Yet he was like a fast baseball team playing on the opponent's watered-down home field; Paul felt he had to play the game by their rules.

Strength Through Weakness (12:7–13)

Paul then turned his thoughts to the deeper truths of God—suffering, unanswered prayer, grace, power, and strength through weakness. While Paul could have become a travel companion of these self-appointed super apostles on their ego trip, he chose instead to follow the road less traveled.

He interpreted his "thorn in my flesh" (12:7) to be a gift that helped him avoid getting conceited. His suffering, his "torment" (12:7), is not named. Through the centuries, interpreters have offered everything from a chronic condition to epilepsy to malaria to depression to eye disease.

Boasting about our human exploits is foolishness.

Whatever it was, Paul cited three times when he "pleaded with the Lord to take it away" (12:8). "Three times" implies that his focused prayers were separate occasions. Possibly there were years between his pleadings. If you have pleaded with the Lord to take away some burden or torment in your life, and your prayer has not been answered, you may want to consider how Paul interpreted his unanswered prayer.

Paul understood the Lord to be saying to him, "My grace is sufficient for you, for my power is made perfect in weakness" (12:9). Was this merely a rationalization of a situation Paul could not change? The cynic and unbeliever would be satisfied with such an answer. But, for the believer, for the follower of Christ who understands discipleship to be taking up the cross daily and following Jesus Christ, this is more than rationalization. This is a lifestyle.

If you have pleaded with the Lord to take away some burden or torment in your life, and your prayer has not been answered, be encouraged. You are in good company with the Apostle Paul and with Christ. With company like that, you can "boast all the more gladly" (12:9) about

"Visions and Revelations"

He is a stable citizen, an ordinary man with an average job who never does a thing to draw attention his way. He is neither self-centered nor flamboyant.

Twenty-five years ago, he had a heart attack. The paramedics and emergency room doctors worked with him and brought him back from death. This man doesn't talk about it much. He won't describe all the details. He just says, "I saw some things. If you are a Christian, you do not need to be afraid of dying."

What do you think about this experience? Do you know anyone with a similar experience?

your weaknesses. Like Paul, you can "delight in weaknesses, in insults, in persecutions, in difficulties" (12:10). You will find that through the sufficient grace of God, it is your weaknesses that make you strong in the power of God.

In 12:11–13, Paul made a transition before he announced in 12:14 his plan to visit them. These words of transition include a tongue-in-cheek apology for writing as a fool, although he is sure to point out that it was their fault (12:11). They should have been commending him, supporting him, and defending him to the self-appointed "super apostles" in Corinth (12:11). Yet, he repeated, he was "nothing" (12:11). The Christians in Corinth could have told the "super-apostles" about his signs, wonders, and miracles done among them. But evidently they were silent (12:12).

The way to wisdom and power is to trust in the Lord so that the peace of God rules in our hearts.

Then, Paul pointed out that the only thing he ever offered to other churches that he never offered to the Corinthian church was the opportunity for them to give him money (12:13). In your imagination, you can see Paul, with a glint in a friendly eye, asking for their forgiveness for never asking them to pay his bills. By implication, he was saying that the "super-apostles" had not avoided this error in judgment.

Implications for Today

In 2 Corinthians 12, Paul instructs us to focus on the strength of God. To focus on the world that is seen with our human eyes and the strengths of our human bodies is nothing compared to the powerful realities of God's kingdom. Boasting about our human exploits is foolishness. The way to wisdom and power is to trust in the Lord so that the peace of God rules in our hearts. God even uses our human sufferings to show us how God's grace is sufficient.

God even uses our human sufferings to show us how God's grace is sufficient.

Remember the ancient saying quoted at the beginning of this lesson: "When a thorn pierces your foot, your whole body must bend over to pull it out."

QUESTIONS

1. Whom do you know who is a living reminder to you that God's grace is sufficient?

2. Do you agree with the words of Gail Neal that are quoted under "Visions and Revelations from the Lord (12:1)"? What are the implications of her words for your life and the life of your church?

3. How is your life spiritually formed by God's visions and revelations in your life?

4. If you have ever written out or verbally presented your testimony, what did you learn from the experience? How might reflecting on your spiritual autobiography influence you to take ministry personally?

5. What are your ideas about heaven?

6. How do your weaknesses make you strong in the Lord?

NOTES

1. Gail M. Neal, "Kingdom Culture Churches," *The Gospel and Our Culture*, monthly newsletter of The Gospel and Our Culture Network, June, 1999.

Focal Text

2 Corinthians
12:14—13:14

Background

2 Corinthians
12:14—13:14

Main Idea

Trying to change people
about whom we are
concerned requires a
delicate combination
of love and wisdom.

Question to
Explore

How can people about
whom we are concerned
be led to change?

Study Aim

To describe how Paul sought to lead the
Corinthians to change and to evaluate whether
and how these methods would be appropriate in
my relationships

Study and Action Emphases

- Affirm the Bible as our authoritative guide for
  life and ministry
- Develop a growing, vibrant faith
- Value all people as created in the image of God
- Encourage healthy families
- Obey and serve Jesus by meeting physical,
  spiritual, and emotional needs
- Equip people for servant leadership

LESSON
THIRTEEN

On Trying to
Change People

Quick Read

As you take ministry personally, you may desire
to change other people; but this is impossible.
Yet, there are some things you can do to nurture
change.

The congregation had been through a two-year interim between pastors. The church leaders were ready for the Pastor Search Committee to complete their work. Yet, the ministry of the church had been guided well over the intervening months. A variety of people had stepped forward to serve. The pastoral staff had provided excellent leadership in coordinating, planning, communicating, and caring.

On the day the Pastor Search Committee announced they were presenting a candidate to the church, there was excitement, anticipation, and anxiety. A new pastor means change.

At a breakfast meeting, the new pastor introduced himself to the pastoral staff. After some pleasantries and general conversations around the breakfast table, the group moved to a room with sofas and overstuffed chairs. The new pastor spoke to them as a group for the first time:

> I want you to know how much I appreciate and value all you have done over the past several years in this church. You have invested yourselves in excellent ministry during the past two years. Interim ministry is hard work. Waiting for a new pastor is stressful. Wondering how your call to ministry, your approach to your own areas of ministry, and your theology of ministry will match with the new pastor is an unknown—especially in these days in Baptist life. Then you have to consider other practical matters like relational style, communication style, personality, etc. So let me say three things to you that we will build on in the future years.
>
> First, you have been here. I have not. I will need you to help me know these people, their needs, and their gifts for ministry. Since this congregation belongs to God and not to us, we are stewards of this church's ministry. We are partners in ministry—partners with Christ, these people, and one another.
>
> Second, this church is becoming what we are being. If we are competitive, territorial, non-trusting, non-communicative, isolated, cliquish, judgmental, and backbiting, this church— these people—will become that way. On the other hand, if we are cooperative, flexible, trusting, open, supportive, sensitive, affirming, and encouraging, these people will become that way. I commit to you that I will live, in my relationship with you, according to the spirit of Christ. I understand my role to be one of exemplary personal influence through personal

integrity, Christian character, and professional competence. I will be your biggest fan and will continually encourage you and this church to invest in your continued development to become all you can become in Christ.

Third, I strongly believe that church health is the soil in which church growth happens. The health of this church is in our hands. Our purpose is to care for the soil, the context, in which this church exists. The people, resources, challenges and opportunities of this church must never be taken for granted. As partners in ministry, we will focus on the health of this church, believing that a healthy church grows spiritually, relationally, missionally, organizationally, and numerically. I look forward to the years ahead. Now, I am done with the sermon. What do you want to talk about?

2 Corinthians 12:14—13:14

[14]Now I am ready to visit you for the third time, and I will not be a burden to you, because what I want is not your possessions but you. After all, children should not have to save up for their parents, but parents for their children. [15]So I will very gladly spend for you everything I have and expend myself as well. If I love you more, will you love me less? [16]Be that as it may, I have not been a burden to you. Yet, crafty fellow that I am, I caught you by trickery! [17]Did I exploit you through any of the men I sent you? [18]I urged Titus to go to you and I sent our brother with him. Titus did not exploit you, did he? Did we not act in the same spirit and follow the same course?

[19]Have you been thinking all along that we have been defending ourselves to you? We have been speaking in the sight of God as those in Christ; and everything we do, dear friends, is for your strengthening. [20]For I am afraid that when I come I may not find you as I want you to be, and you may not find me as you want me to be. I fear that there may be quarreling, jealousy, outbursts of anger, factions, slander, gossip, arrogance and disorder. [21]I am afraid that when I come again my God will humble me before you, and I will be grieved over many who have sinned earlier and have not repented of the impurity, sexual sin and debauchery in which they have indulged.

[13:1]This will be my third visit to you. "Every matter must be established by the testimony of two or three witnesses." [2]I already gave you a warning when I was with you the second time. I now repeat it while absent: On my return I will not spare those who sinned earlier or any of the others, [3]since you are demanding proof that Christ is speaking through me. He is not weak in dealing with you, but is powerful among you. [4]For to be sure, he was crucified in weakness, yet he lives by God's power. Likewise, we are weak in him, yet by God's power we will live with him to serve you.

[5]Examine yourselves to see whether you are in the faith; test yourselves. Do you not realize that Christ Jesus is in you—unless, of course, you fail the test? [6]And I trust that you will discover that we have not failed the test. [7]Now we pray to God that you will not do anything wrong. Not that people will see that we have stood the test but that you will do what is right even though we may seem to have failed. [8]For we cannot do anything against the truth, but only for the truth. [9]We are glad whenever we are weak but you are strong; and our prayer is for your perfection. [10]This is why I write these things when I am absent, that when I come I may not have to be harsh in my use of authority—the authority the Lord gave me for building you up, not for tearing you down.

[11]Finally, brothers, good-by. Aim for perfection, listen to my appeal, be of one mind, live in peace. And the God of love and peace will be with you.

[12]Greet one another with a holy kiss. [13]All the saints send their greetings.

[14]May the grace of the Lord Jesus Christ, and the love of God, and the fellowship of the Holy Spirit be with you all.

Get the Guest Room Ready (12:14a)

Like a parent who calls to tell the adult children, *I'm coming to see you*, Paul told the Corinthian church of his plans for a third visit. His first visit, probably around A.D. 51–53, is described in Acts 18. That passage tells of how he lived with Aquilla and Priscilla and worked with them in their tent-making business. Every Saturday (Sabbath day), he went to the synagogue, trying to persuade Jews and Greeks to follow Christ. After Silas and Timothy arrived from Macedonia, Paul devoted himself exclusively to preaching Christ. But the Jews became abusive, and so he left the synagogue and went next door to the home of Titius Justus, a worshiper of God. Crispus, who was the ruler of the synagogue, and his entire household believed in Christ and were baptized. After hearing the Lord tell him to have bold faith and not fear, since the Lord had many people in that city who needed Paul's teaching, Paul stayed for a year and a half. Then he left and went on to Ephesus for a short visit.

In between his first and second visits, Paul wrote to the Corinthian church what is called the "lost letter," mentioned in 1 Corinthians 5:9. Soon after this, the church in Corinth wrote to Paul (see 1 Corinthians 7:1) about several issues. Then some people from Chloe's household informed Paul about some quarrels in the church related to territorialism and shallow loyalties to different teachers and leaders (1 Cor. 1:11). (You know, things like, *I can't move into that class where Apollos teaches. I am in Cephas's class.*)

During about A.D. 54–55, Paul wrote what we know as 1 Corinthians, which was actually his second letter to Corinth. Later that same year, Paul made his second visit to Corinth (2 Cor. 2:1). This second visit was brief, due to opposition to him plus divisions within the church. My view is that it was after this visit that he wrote 2 Corinthians 10—13, his third letter to them, in which he proposed he would visit them again. Actually, what Paul said was, "I am ready to visit you" (12:14). He was not sure whether they were ready for his visit. This mention of an impending visit must have whetted their appetite to see him.

> *"Since this congregation belongs to God and not to us, we are stewards of this church's ministry."*

Several months later, Titus met Paul in Macedonia and reported on Corinth (2 Corinthians 7:5–13). Titus told Paul that there were people in Corinth who were concerned for Paul and longed to see him. The report by Titus encouraged Paul. So Paul wrote what we have as 2 Corinthians 1—9, his fourth letter to the Corinthian church. It was after this that he actually made his third and final visit to Corinth mentioned here (12:14).

Paul's notice to the Corinthians that he would like to visit them again prompted them to prepare. Over the ensuing months, they waited and waited. He did not come. This delay created anticipation in the Corinthians and allowed time for God's Holy Spirit to work in their hearts.

Through the intervening months, Paul was transformed from being an unwelcome visitor into an expected guest. *Visitor* is the word we print on scoreboards when we want to defeat someone and send them away losers. *Guest* is the word we use to talk of special towels, special rooms, and specially prepared places at the table of fellowship.

A Hope-full and Fear-full Trip (12:14b–21)

Paul loved the Corinthian church. Like a parent who loves a child, Paul also had some concerns for the Corinthians. He did not desire to be a burden on them (12:14b). He only wanted to express his love for them to them. He wanted nothing from them. He wanted only to focus on his relationship with them and focus on their mutual relationship with Christ. He desired to invest himself in them. He had no interest in their possessions (12:15). Paul had been accused of being crafty and using trickery to exploit the Corinthians financially (12:16–18), a charge he denied.

It is strange that some people immediately connect the ideas of ministry and money. I have actually watched people button their pockets and zip their purses when they realized I was a pastoral person. It is as though some people think these two subjects go together on an analogy test. The question would be like this: *Peanut butter is to jelly as ministry is to* ____ _____? Many people would choose *money* even if the other three options were *reconciliation, service,* and *mission.*

Up until now, Paul had spent this entire letter defending and explaining himself against questions and charges of the Corinthians against him. But the rest of the letter focuses on his concerns for them. He began by explaining that his concern for them is that they would be strengthened in their faith in the Lord (12:19). While he had many hopes for his work and ministry with them, he was aware that some of them might not receive him as a trustworthy representative of Christ. In addition, he had serious concerns and fears about them (12:20–21).

> "The health of this church is in our hands."

Paul was afraid that upon his arrival, he would experience "quarreling, jealousy, outbursts of anger, factions, slander, gossip, arrogance and disorder" (12:20). He was not excited about walking into that type of community. Who would be? That would be like sharing a house with the families of Archie Bunker, Roseanne, and Ozzie Osborne all at the same time.

Furthermore, Paul was afraid that the same unbridled and undisciplined sexual promiscuity was going on among them (12:21). Corinth may very well have been the most cosmopolitan city among the early church contexts. Relational lifestyles that followed the narrow road of Jesus' teachings were not mainstream. Paul feared that many of these people had not repented (made a complete turn-around) in their behaviors.

Paul was reluctant to walk into a church where (1) his integrity and authenticity were being attacked; where (2) a relational community existed only as an organization focused on doctrine, not as a community of faith and love focused on Christ's mission; and where (3) the same self-serving, sinful lifestyles were being pursued that he had challenged in prior years.

Would you be excited about a trip like that? Would you be running right out to pack your suitcase and cash in frequent flyer points?

The Two-Minute Warning (13:1–4)

Like a time-out and commercial at the two-minute mark of a football game, Paul called on the Corinthians to remember that this would be his third visit (13:1). He expected them to have dealt with these issues prior to his arrival. Like a health inspector who has given a bad report to a restaurant, Paul says, *You know what your problems are. So look at them, figure it out, and fix them* (13:2). Just as Paul was being required to make preparations for their next meeting, he made some homework assignments to the Corinthians.

> *The church should always be examining itself to make sure it is living under the authority of Christ.*

The Corinthians were listening to the self-appointed super-apostles as they made fun of the small-framed rabbi who walked short and carried a

Soul Competence

Baptists consider it a foundational principle of our heritage to affirm each person's right to make choices without coercion or manipulation. How can we be instruments for change while honoring the Baptist principle of soul competence?

Change is defined as "a new condition which is self-maintaining."[1] A model for why and how change happens is: $(A + B + C) > D = Change$.[2] This model can be explained as follows:

A represents a significant level of dissatisfaction with some present condition.

B represents an awareness of an alternative better condition.

C represents knowledge of the first steps to take in changing to the better condition.

D represents the costs of making the change.

+ suggests that *A*, *B*, and *C* must be added together as simultaneous factors.

> connotes that the value of *A*, *B*, and *C* must be greater than *D*.

Where do you sense significant levels of dissatisfaction? In these places of dissatisfaction, is there an awareness of a better condition? Too, is there knowledge of the first steps to take to move toward the better condition? What are the costs of making this change? How can you be an influence toward healthy change?

big pen and parchment. Once again, Paul reminded them of the theological puzzle of strength in weakness (13:4).

The Corinthians were so interested in Paul verifying that he was speaking and teaching through the authority of Christ. Paul stressed that this Christ was going to speak and teach and work powerfully among them through Paul (13:3). Paul pointed out that while Jesus may have appeared weak in his crucifixion, Jesus lives today by the power of God. In like manner, while Paul might not compare in looks, superficial power, or oratorical ability to the false apostles, the power of God's Christ would be manifest in little old Paul (13:4).

Get Things Cleaned Up (13:5–10)

The mother walked into the teenager's room and said with intensity, *I want this room cleaned up. I will be back in two hours, and this room had better look different.*

As Paul began to wind down his letter, he wound up his intensity. Basically, he said, *I will be coming to see you. But before I do, you folks have some things to clear up and clean up. And I don't mean to just tidy up for a quick visit. I mean clean from the inside-out, from side to side and bottom to top.*

Paul told them to examine themselves "to see whether you are in the faith" (13:5). In the theology of Paul, faith was not a set of doctrinal creeds or the power to work miracles. For Paul, faith was a relationship with God's Christ that was based on complete trust in Christ and commitment to his mission. The church should always be examining itself to make sure it is living under the authority of Christ.

Paul loved the Corinthians and hoped for a relational community of faith for them.

Paul, though, did not call the Corinthian church to examine itself organizationally, financially, or doctrinally. Rather, he suggested that every believer should do a self-examination. This examination should test their individual relationship with God's Christ.

Paul did not encourage them to examine one another. He did not tell them to write out a set of doctrinal statements and have everyone sign it. Neither did he suggest passing a resolution and publishing it in the *Corinthian Courier*. Paul proposed that they examine whether Christ was in their lives (13:5). Usually, Paul wrote of believers being in Christ. His reference to Christ being in their lives is a reminder that the relationship

Enablers of Change

After you overview the following list, determine which of these initiatives have enabled change in you and which you have used to invite change in others:

- Expressing a desire to spend time with them (12:14)
- Assuring of no desire to be a burden to them (12:15)
- Focusing on investing in a deeper relationship (12:15)
- Reminding them of past times (12:16–18)
- Affirming your interest in their growth (12:19)
- Caring enough to confront them (12:20–21)
- Naming the desired outcome (13:1–4)
- Encouraging self-examination (13:5–8)
- Praying for them (13:9)
- Building them up, not tearing them down (13:10)
- Continuing the relationship (13:11–14)

of the Christian believer with Jesus Christ is mutual—Christ in you and you in Christ.

Paul's Sign-off (13:11–14)

Humorist Garrison Keillor has made Lake Wobegon seem like a real place to millions of people who listen to his weekly public radio show, *A Prairie Home Companion*. Keillor also shows up daily on public radio (and on the internet) with a brief syndicated show called *The Writer's Almanac*. Keillor signs off that show with these words: "Be well, do good work, and keep in touch."[8]

> *. . . The relationship of the Christian believer with Jesus Christ is mutual—Christ in you and you in Christ.*

Translating Paul's sign-off of this correspondence in *Southernese*, we can hear him saying something like this: *Bye now. Y'all do the best you can. Mind what I say. Get along. Do what's right by each other. And the good Lord will be with you. Treat each other good. Everybody here says hi.*

Paul loved the Corinthians and hoped for a relational community of faith for them. He continued to exemplify humility, honesty, authenticity, and vulnerability in the last words of the letter.

Implications for Us

Paul took his ministry personally. He became frustrated by other people who chose to live according to their own authority rather than as fully devoted followers of Christ. He desired to see people change who were shallow in their spiritual commitment and were easily drawn off track by manipulative self-appointed religious superstars. But Paul knew the best he could do was to live his life according to the spirit and character of Christ and pray that the Corinthians would desire to change and decide to change as a result of his example.

> *. . . Paul knew the best he could do was to live his life according to the spirit and character of Christ and pray that the Corinthians would . . . decide to change as a result of his example.*

As you take ministry personally, you may desire to change other people, but this is impossible. You can only become the change you desire to see in them and nurture a relational environment that makes it safe for them to change.

QUESTIONS

1. How does the relationship between your pastoral staff and church leadership set the tone for congregational health and growth? If you do not sense healthy relationships among the leaders, how may your class be a stimulus by becoming the change you would hope to see?

2. When a person comes to your church or class for the first time, how do you make sure they have the experience of a *guest* and not that of a *visitor*? Do you expect guests each week? What preparations have you made for them?

3. Why do you think some churches seem so focused on quarreling, jealousy, outbursts of anger, factions, slander, gossip, arrogance, and disorder? Do you think these are truly communities of Christian faith and mission, or are they merely social organizations with a church sign out front?

4. Why do you think we are so prone to evaluate a person's capacity to be an influential Christian leader based on the person's looks, stature, position, oratorical ability, academic degrees, collegial network, etc.? What should we look for?

5. How do you examine yourself as to whether Christ is in you? How do you help others in your family know how to examine themselves as to whether they are hosting Christ in their heart?

6. Do you find that self-appointed super religious leaders often fail to reflect the characteristics of humility, honesty, authenticity, and vulnerability? If so, why do you think these folks have so many followers?

NOTES

1. Elaine Dickson, *Say No, Say Yes to Change* (Nashville, Tennessee: Broadman Press, 1982), 52.
2. See Dickson, 26.

Our Next New Study

(Available for use beginning December 2004)

THE GOSPEL OF MATTHEW: *Jesus' Teachings*

UNIT FIVE, TEACHINGS ABOUT ACCOUNTABILITY

Additional Resources for Studying the Teachings of Jesus in Matthew[1]

Craig L. Blomberg. *Matthew.* The New American Commentary. Nashville: Broadman Press, 1992.

Dietrich Bonhoeffer. *The Cost of Discipleship.* New York: Simon & Schuster, Touchstone Book, 1995 (originally published in German in 1937).

M. Eugene Boring. "Matthew." *The New Interpreter's Bible.* Nashville: Abingdon Press, 1995.

David Garland. *Reading Matthew.* Macon, Georgia: Smyth and Helwys Publishing, Inc., 1999.

Douglas R. A. Hare. *Matthew.* Interpretation: A Bible Commentary for Teaching and Preaching. Louisville: John Knox Press, 1993.

Clarence Jordan, *The Cotton Patch Version of Matthew and John.* Piscataway, New Jersey: New Century Publishers, Inc., 1970.

Clarence Jordan. *The Sermon on the Mount.* Revised edition. Valley Forge: Judson Press, Koinonia Edition, 1970.

Frank Stagg. "Matthew." *The Broadman Bible Commentary.* Volume 8. Nashville: Broadman Press, 1969.

NOTES

1. Listing a book does not imply full agreement by the writers or BAPTISTWAY PRESS® with all of its comments.

How to Order More Bible Study Materials

It's easy! Just fill in the following information. (Note: when the *Teaching Guide* is priced at $1.95, the *Teaching Guide* contains only teaching plans.)♣ = Texas specific

Title of item	Price	Quantity	Cost
This Issue:			
2 Corinthians: Taking Ministry Personally—Study Guide	$2.35	_____	_____
2 Corinthians: Taking Ministry Personally—Large Print Study Guide	$2.35	_____	_____
2 Corinthians: Taking Ministry Personally—Teaching Guide	$2.95	_____	_____
Previous Issues Available:			
God's Message in the Old Testament—Study Guide♣	$1.95	_____	_____
God's Message in the Old Testament—Teaching Guide♣	$1.95	_____	_____
Genesis 12—50: Family Matters—Study Guide	$1.95	_____	_____
Genesis 12—50: Family Matters—Large Print Study Guide	$1.95	_____	_____
Genesis 12—50: Family Matters—Teaching Guide	$2.45	_____	_____
Exodus: Freed to Follow God—Study Guide	$2.35	_____	_____
Exodus: Freed to Follow God—Large Print Study Guide	$2.35	_____	_____
Exodus: Freed to Follow God—Teaching Guide	$2.95	_____	_____
Isaiah and Jeremiah—Study Guide	$1.95	_____	_____
Isaiah and Jeremiah—Large Print Study Guide	$1.95	_____	_____
Isaiah and Jeremiah—Teaching Guide	$2.45	_____	_____
Amos, Hosea, Micah—Study Guide	$1.95	_____	_____
Amos, Hosea, Micah—Teaching Guide	$2.45	_____	_____
Good News in the New Testament—Study Guide♣	$1.95	_____	_____
Good News in the New Testament—Large Print Study Guide♣	$1.95	_____	_____
Good News in the New Testament—Teaching Guide♣	$2.45	_____	_____
Matthew: Jesus As the Fulfillment of God's Promises— Study Guide♣	$1.00	_____	_____
Matthew: Jesus As the Fulfillment of God's Promises— Large Print Study Guide♣	$1.00	_____	_____
Matthew: Jesus As the Fulfillment of God's Promises— Teaching Guide♣	$2.00	_____	_____
Jesus in the Gospel of Mark—Study Guide	$1.95	_____	_____
Jesus in the Gospel of Mark—Large Print Study Guide	$1.95	_____	_____
Jesus in the Gospel of Mark—Teaching Guide	$2.45	_____	_____
Luke: Parables Jesus Told—Study Guide	$2.35	_____	_____
Luke: Parables Jesus Told—Large Print Study Guide	$2.35	_____	_____
Luke: Parables Jesus Told—Teaching Guide	$2.95	_____	_____
Gospel of John—Study Guide	$1.95	_____	_____
Gospel of John—Teaching Guide	$2.45	_____	_____
Acts: Sharing God's Good News with Everyone—Study Guide♣	$1.95	_____	_____
Acts: Sharing God's Good News with Everyone— Teaching Guide♣	$1.95	_____	_____
Romans: Good News for a Troubled World—Study Guide♣	$1.95	_____	_____
Romans: Good News for a Troubled World—Teaching Guide♣	$1.95	_____	_____
1 Corinthians—Study Guide	$1.95	_____	_____
1 Corinthians—Large Print Study Guide	$1.95	_____	_____
1 Corinthians—Teaching Guide	$2.45	_____	_____
Galatians and Ephesians—Study Guide♣	$1.95	_____	_____
Galatians and Ephesians—Large Print Study Guide♣	$1.95	_____	_____
Galatians and Ephesians—Teaching Guide♣	$2.45	_____	_____
Philippians, Colossians, Thessalonians—Teaching Guide	$2.45	_____	_____
Hebrews and James—Study Guide	$1.95	_____	_____
Hebrews and James—Large Print Study Guide	$1.95	_____	_____
Hebrews and James—Teaching Guide	$2.45	_____	_____
Letters of John and Peter—Study Guide	$1.95	_____	_____
Letters of John and Peter—Large Print Study Guide	$1.95	_____	_____
Letters of John and Peter—Teaching Guide	$2.45	_____	_____

Coming for use beginning December 2004

Matthew: Jesus' Teachings—Study Guide	$2.35	_____	_____
Matthew: Jesus' Teachings—Large Print Study Guide	$2.35	_____	_____
Matthew: Jesus' Teachings—Teaching Guide	$2.95	_____	_____

Beliefs Important to Baptists

Who in the World Are Baptists, Anyway? (one lesson)	$ .45	_____	_____
Who in the World Are Baptists, Anyway?—Teacher's Edition	$ .55	_____	_____
Beliefs Important to Baptists: I (four lessons)	$1.35	_____	_____
Beliefs Important to Baptists: I—Teacher's Edition	$1.75	_____	_____
Beliefs Important to Baptists: II (four lessons)	$1.35	_____	_____
Beliefs Important to Baptists: II—Teacher's Edition	$1.75	_____	_____
Beliefs Important to Baptists: III (four lessons)	$1.35	_____	_____
Beliefs Important to Baptists: III—Teacher's Edition	$1.75	_____	_____
Beliefs Important to Baptists—Study Guide (one-volume edition; includes all lessons)	$2.35	_____	_____
Beliefs Important to Baptists—Teaching Guide (one-volume edition; includes all lessons)	$1.95	_____	_____

---

*Charges for standard shipping service:

Subtotal up to $20.00	$3.95
Subtotal $20.01—$50.00	$4.95
Subtotal $50.01—$100.00	10% of subtotal
Subtotal $100.01 and up	8% of subtotal

Please allow three weeks for standard delivery. For express shipping service: Call 1–866–249–1799 for information on additional charges.

Subtotal _____

Shipping* _____

TOTAL _____

Your name   Phone

Your church   Date Ordered

Mailing address

City   State   Zip code

MAIL this form with your check for the total amount to
BAPTISTWAY PRESS
Baptist General Convention of Texas
333 North Washington
Dallas, TX 75246-1798
(Make checks to "Baptist Executive Board.")

OR, **FAX** your order anytime to: 214-828-5187, and we will bill you.

OR, **CALL** your order toll-free: 1-866-249-1799 (8:30 a.m.-5:00 p.m., M-F), and we will bill you.

OR, **E-MAIL** your order to our internet e-mail address: baptistway@bgct.org, and we will bill you.

We look forward to receiving your order! Thank you!